KB236091

Phonics PARTY 2

Short Vowel Sounds

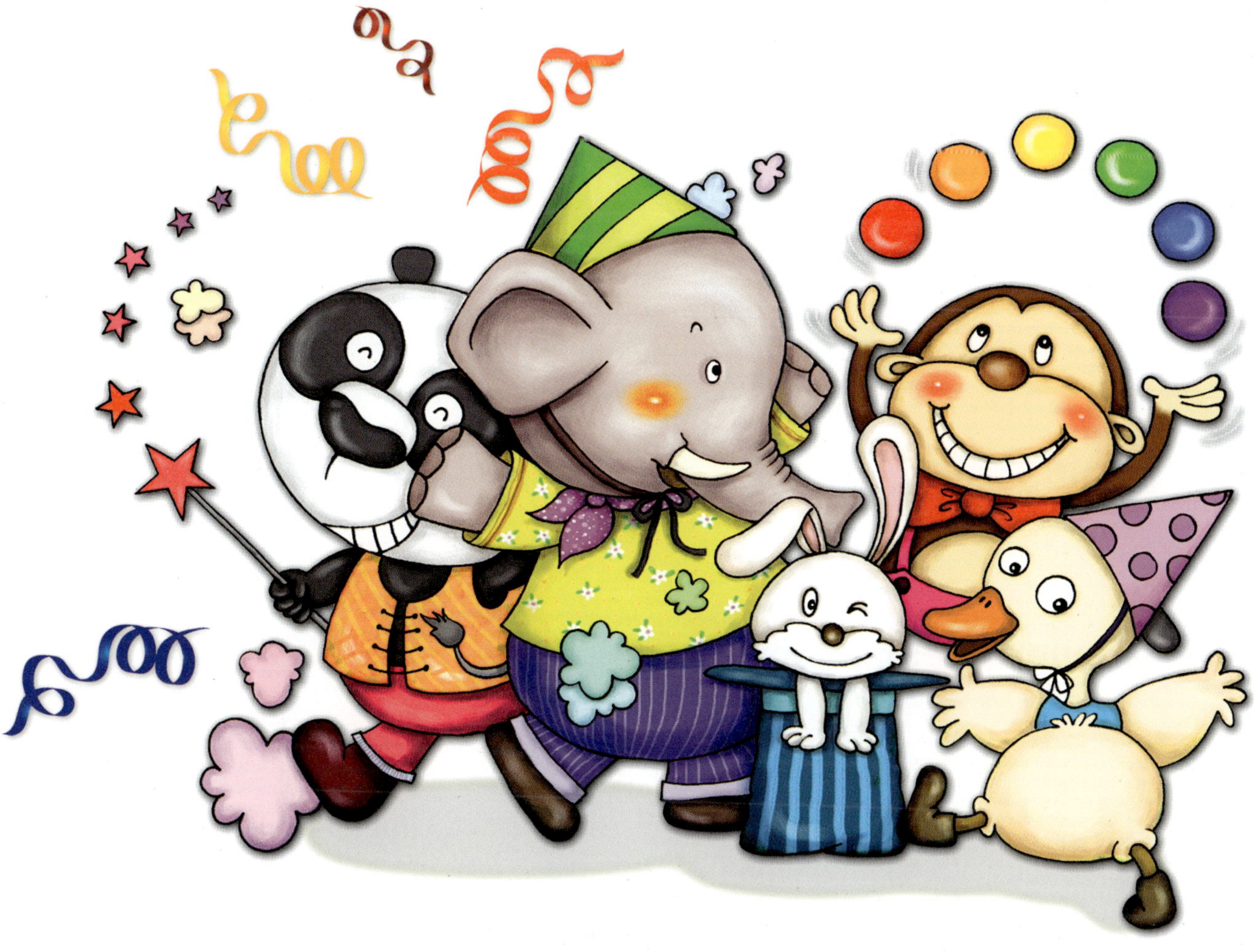

WorldCom Edu

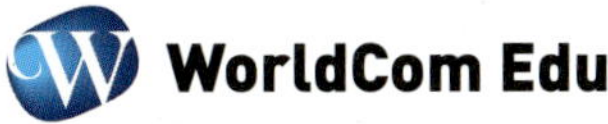

CONTENTS

Short vowel a

-ad   -ag

🎧 Listen and repeat. 📄 **01** / Unit 1

| bad | dad | sad |

| bag | tag | wag |

Date　　　.　　.　　.

2. Write

🎧 Listen, put on the stickers, and write. MP3 **02** / Unit 1

dad

mad

rag

✏️ Match the words to the pictures.

tag ·

· 

dad ·

· 

sad ·

.MP3 03 / Unit 1

🎧 Listen and circle the pictures that rhyme with "tag".

.MP3 04 / Unit 1

🎧 Listen and circle the pictures that rhyme with "dad".

Date　　　　.　　.　　.

4. Practice

🎧 **Listen and circle the correct pictures.** 🎵 **05** / Unit 1

1 

2 

3 

4 

✏️ **Circle and write.**

w**ag**

d ______

s ______

b ______

Listen and match the words to the pictures. **06** / Unit 1

1 I have a bag. •   • 

2 My dad is mad. •   • 

3 The boy is sad. •   • 

4 This is a tag. •   • 

Date . . .

6. Homework

✏️ Unscramble the words and read.

g a t

tag

g a w

g a b

d a d

m a d

a d b

d s a

g r a

Short vowel a

-am   -an

 1. Listen

🎧 Listen and repeat. **07** / Unit 2

 a **+**  m **➡** am

ham   jam   ram

 a **+**  n **➡** an

  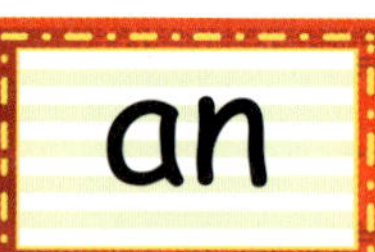

can   fan   pan

  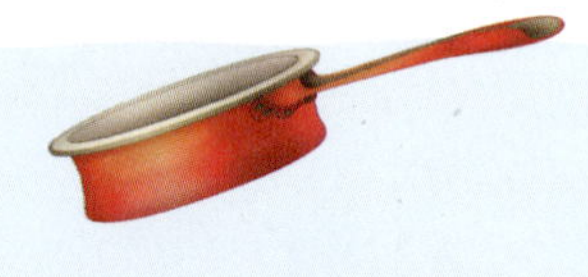

Date   .   .   .

2. Write

Listen, put on the stickers, and write. **08** / Unit 2

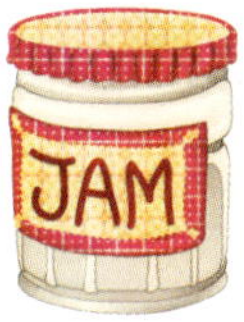

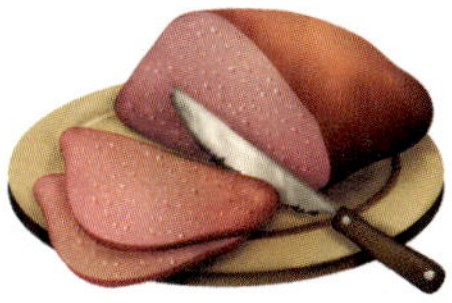

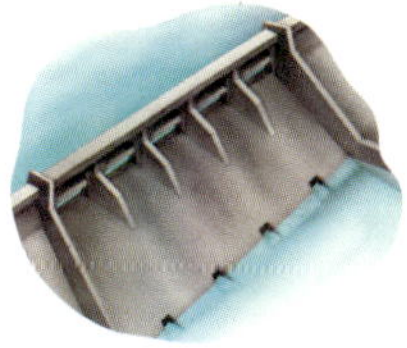

dam

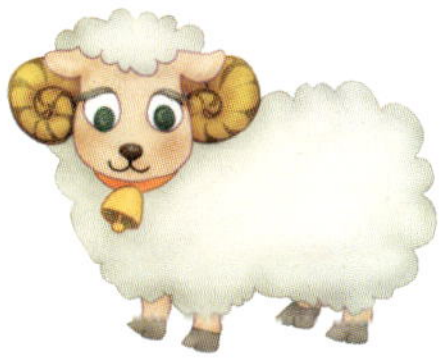

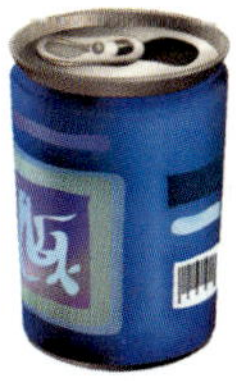

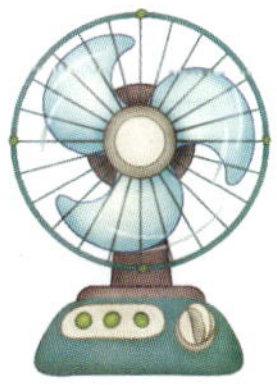

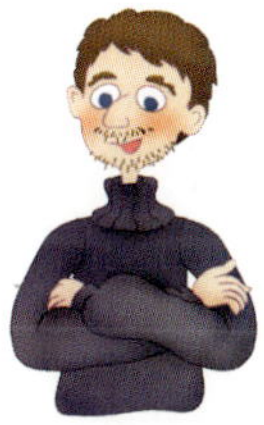

man

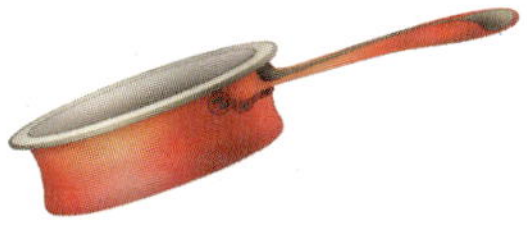

Match the words to the pictures.

man •

dam •

pan •

.MP3 **09** / Unit 2

Listen and circle the pictures that rhyme with "jam".

.MP3 **10** / Unit 2

Listen and circle the pictures that rhyme with "pan".

   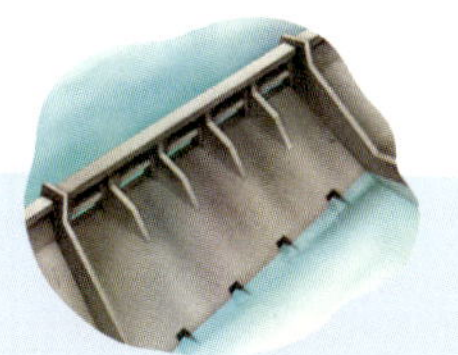

Date　　　.　　.　　.

4. Practice

🎧 Listen and circle the correct pictures. **11** / Unit 2

1

2

3

4

✏️ Circle and write.

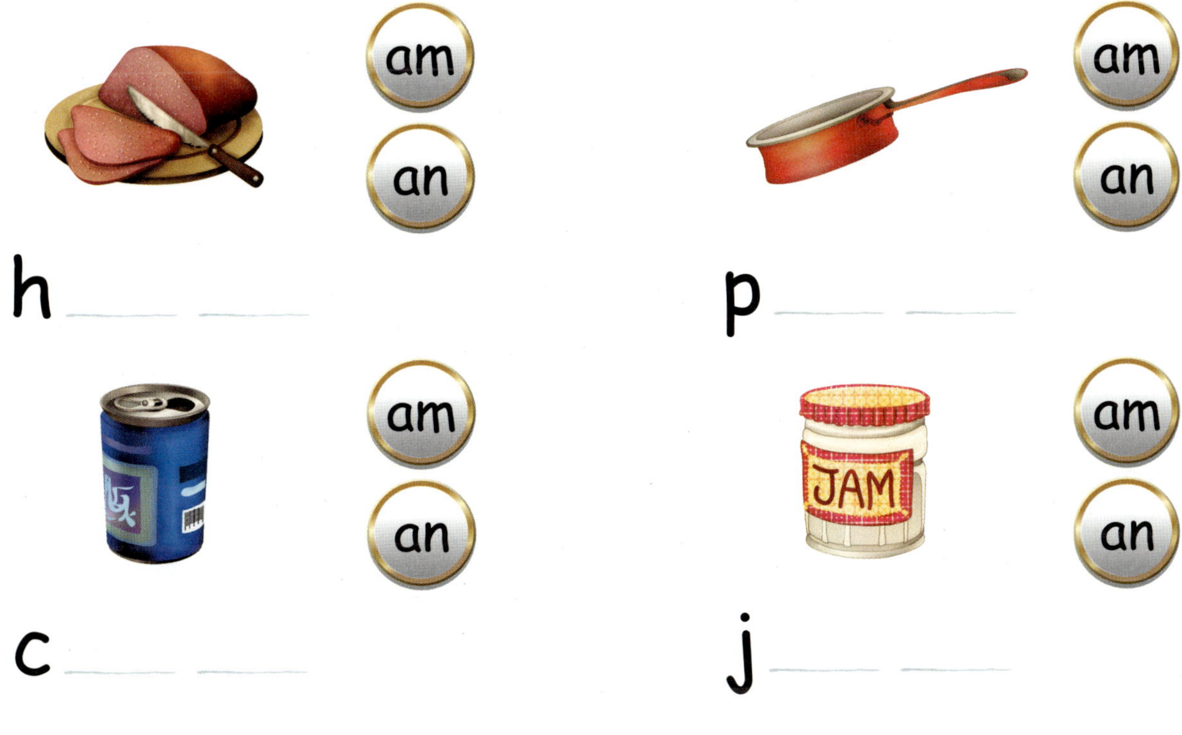

h ______

am
an

p ______

am
an

c ______

am
an

j ______

am
an

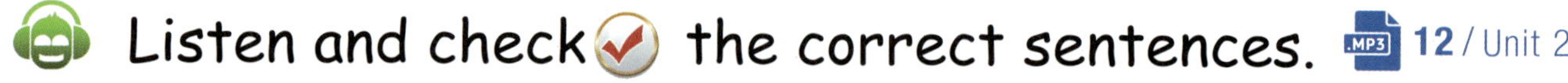

Listen and check ✓ the correct sentences. **.MP3** **12** / Unit 2

1

- ○ Sam has a dam.
- ✓ Sam has a ham.

2

- ○ The fan is on the pan.
- ○ The can is on the pan.

3

- ○ The man has a pan.
- ○ The man has a fan.

4

- ○ The ram has a ham.
- ○ The ram has some jam.

Date　　　　.　　.　　.

6. Homework

 Write and circle the correct words.

jam

j a n m j a m n a j 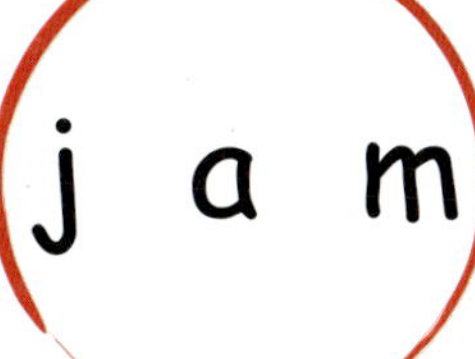

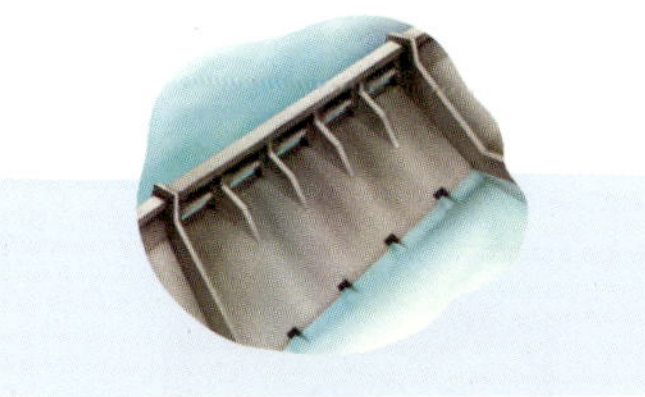

n f a n f n m a f a

m d n m a n d d a m

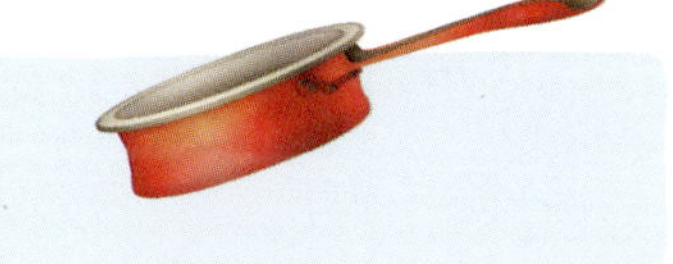

p a p a n m a p n a

Short vowel a

-ap   -at

PP2-03
MP3

🎧 Listen and repeat.  **13** / Unit 3

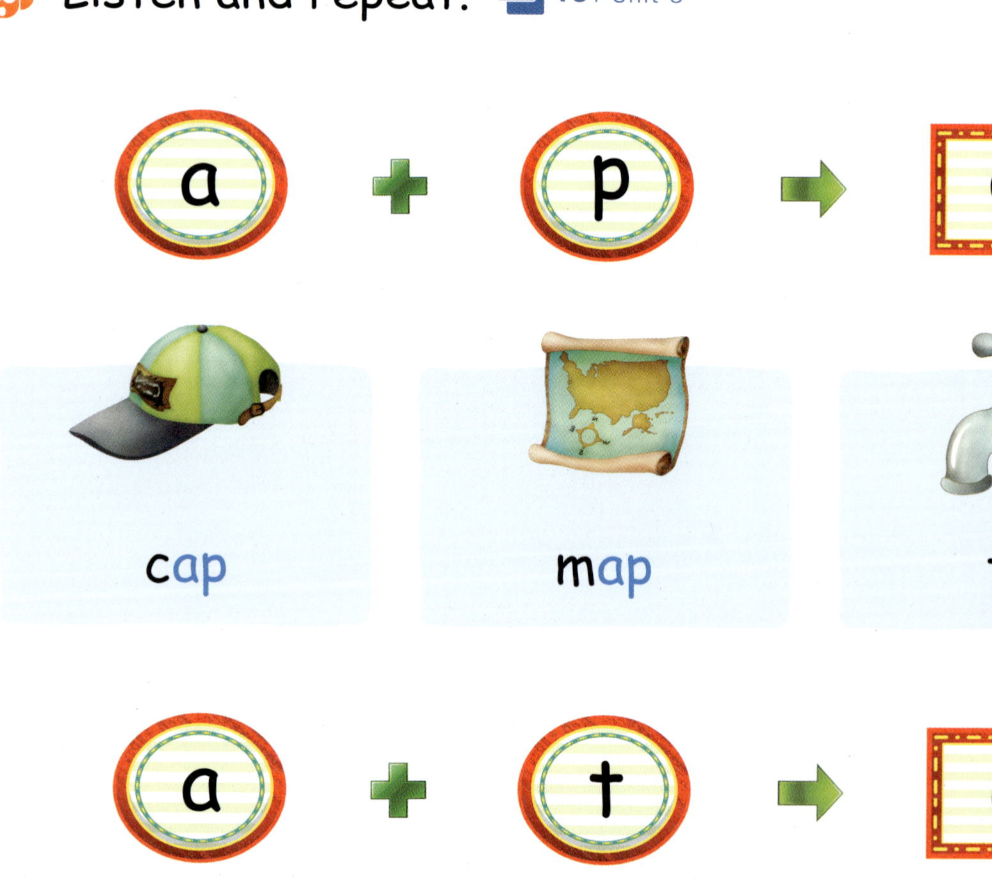

| a | + | p | → | ap |

cap

map

tap

| a | + | t | → | at |

cat

hat

mat

Date . . .

2. Write

Listen, put on the stickers, and write. MP3 14 / Unit 3

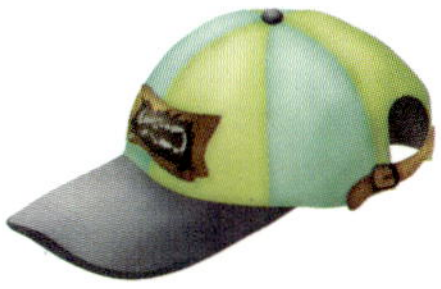

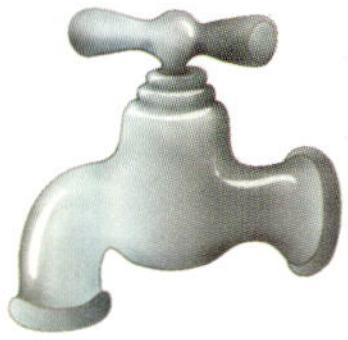

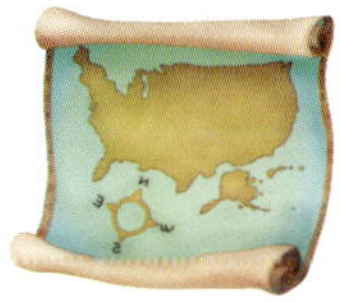

lap

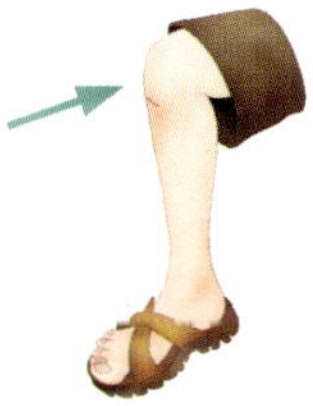

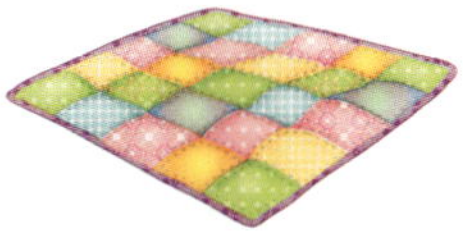

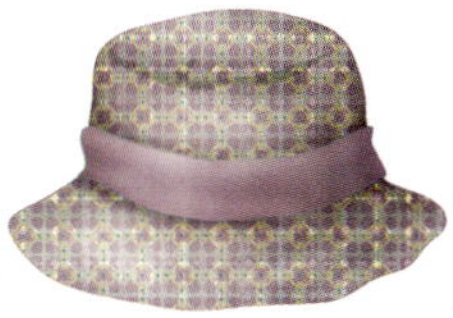

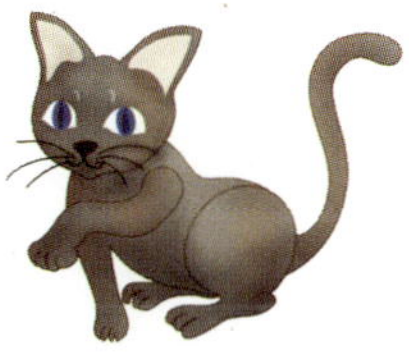

bat

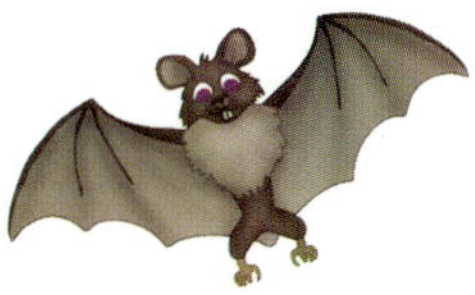

3. Learn

✏️ Match the words to the pictures.

mat •

cap •

map •

📄 **15** / Unit 3

🎧 Listen and circle the pictures that rhyme with "map".

📄 **16** / Unit 3

🎧 Listen and circle the pictures that rhyme with "mat".

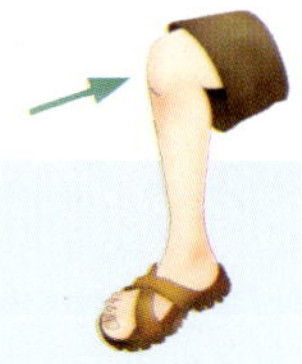         

Date   .   .   .

4. Practice

🎧 Listen and circle the correct pictures. 📄 **17** / Unit 3

1 

2

3 

4 

✏️ Circle and write.

ap
at

c _______

ap
at

m _______

ap
at

c _______

ap
at

m _______

Listen and check ✓ the correct sentences. **MP3 18** / Unit 3

1

2

The cat is on the lap. 　The cap is on the tap.

The cat is on the map. 　The cap is on the map.

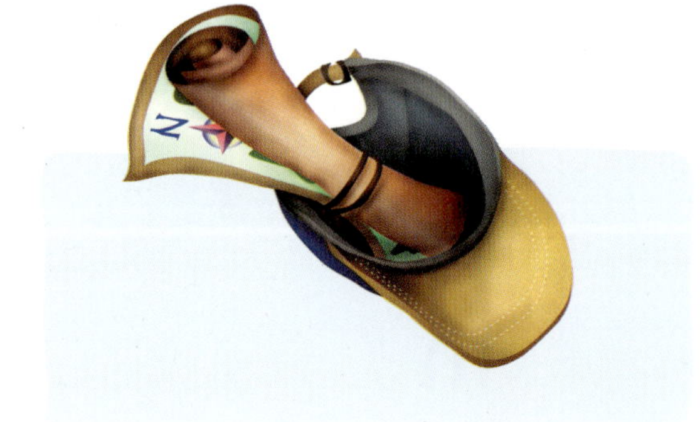

3

4

The map is in the cap. 　The hat is on the mat.

The map is in the tap. 　The bat is on the mat.

Date ____________ . ____ . ____

6. Homework

✏ **Write the words. Then match the words that rhyme.**

Short vowel a

PP2-R-1
MP3

 Listen and complete the words. 19 / Review 1

1		c ·	· ag
2		s ·	· am
3		c ·	· at
4		t ·	· ad
5		m ·	· ap
6		h ·	· an

Date　　.　　.　　.

✏️ Find the words. ↓ → ↘ ↑

| fan | sad | map | wag | mat | ram |

f	e	n	m	a	p
d	r	f	e	a	n
n	s	a	r	m	t
a	d	n	m	p	e
m	a	g	h	t	m
f	s	w	a	g	n

Find these words on the picture and circle.

 **Listen and repeat.**  **20** / Review 1

1. My dad is not sad, mad or bad.

2. Wag the rag or the bag with the tag.

3. The ram eats ham with jam on a dam.

4. The man has a can and a fan on a pan.

5. The cap, tap, and map are on my lap.

6. A bat and cat wear a hat on a mat.

Listen and write the words. **.MP3** **21** / Review 1

1 ________________   6 ________________

2 ________________   7 ________________

3 ________________   8 ________________

4 ________________   9 ________________

5 ________________   10 ________________

Score ________________

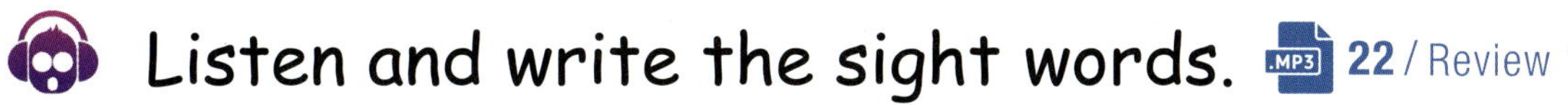

Listen and write the sight words. MP3 **22** / Review 1

1 are

2 what

3 has

4 was

Find the sight words. ↓ → ↘ ↑

| are |
| what |
| has |
| was |

c	l	s	e	d
a	w	a	s	i
r	v	h	j	a
e	b	t	a	f
k	l	s	y	t

Short vowel e

-ed   -eg

PP2-04
MP3

Listen and repeat. **23** / Unit 4

e + d → ed

bed

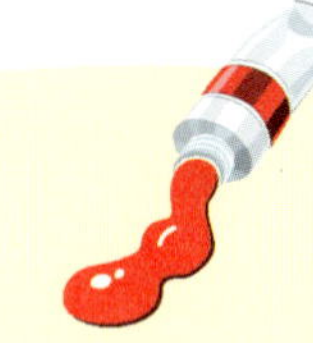
red

Ted

e + g → eg

beg

leg

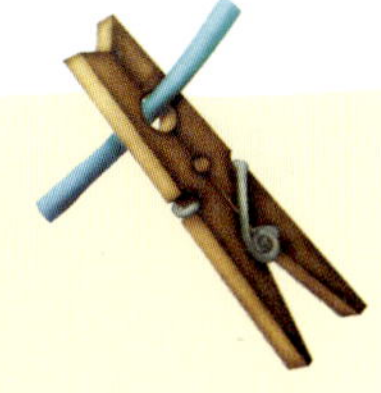
peg

Date   .   .   .

2. Write

 Listen, put on the stickers, and write. .MP3 **24** / Unit 4

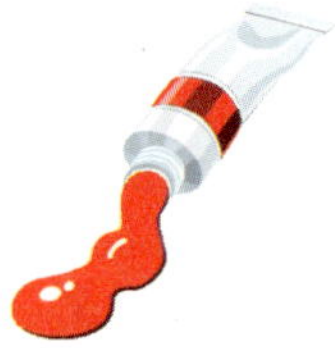

wed

egg

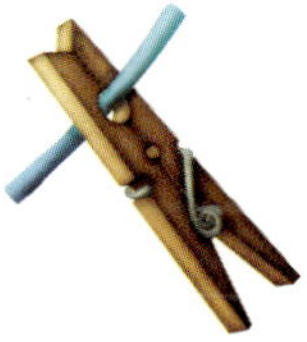

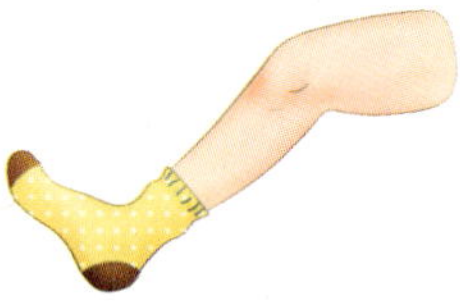

Match the words to the pictures.

leg •

red •

peg •

25 / Unit 4

Listen and circle the pictures that rhyme with "leg".

26 / Unit 4

Listen and circle the pictures that rhyme with "bed".

Date . . .

4. Practice

🎧 Listen and circle the correct pictures. 📁 **27** / Unit 4

1

2

3

4

✏️ Circle and write.

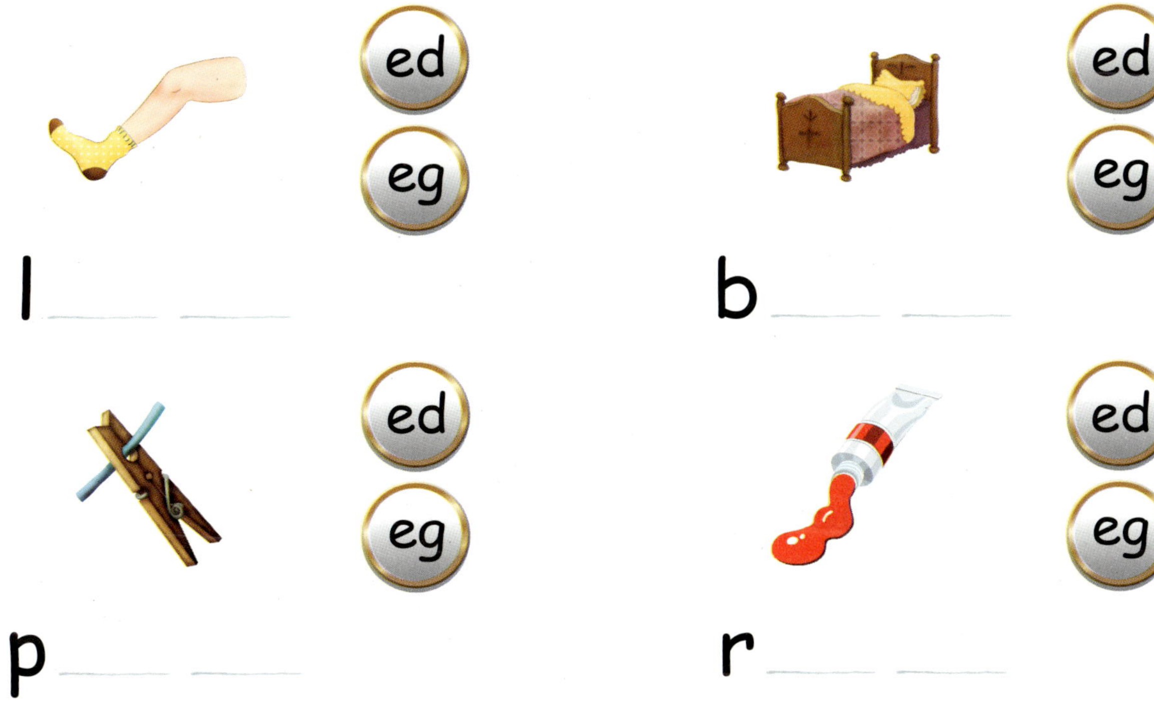

ed
eg

l _______

ed
eg

b _______

ed
eg

p _______

ed
eg

r _______

Circle the words in the box. ↓ →

a	p	c	e	r	b
T	e	d	r	e	t
e	g	b	e	d	a
p	e	o	e	g	g
l	e	g	b	a	d
r	e	e	t	o	l

bed   peg   Ted   red   egg   leg

Date　　.　　.　　.

6. Homework

Look and circle. Does the picture have a "short e" sound?

UNIT 5

Short vowel e

-en -et

PP2-05
MP3

🎧 Listen and repeat.  **28** / Unit 5

e + n ➡ en

hen

pen

10
ten

e + t ➡ et

net

pet

wet

Date   .   .   .

2. Write

 Listen, put on the stickers, and write. **29** / Unit 5

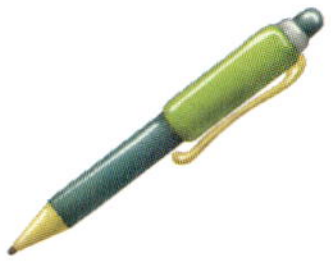

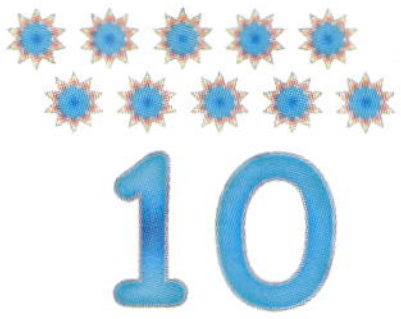

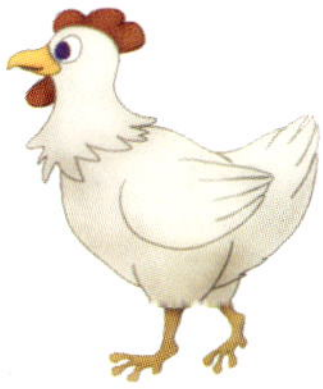

men

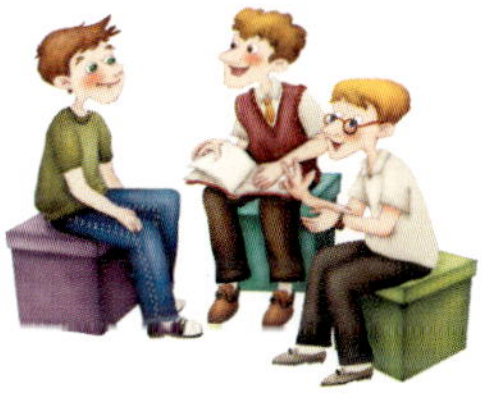

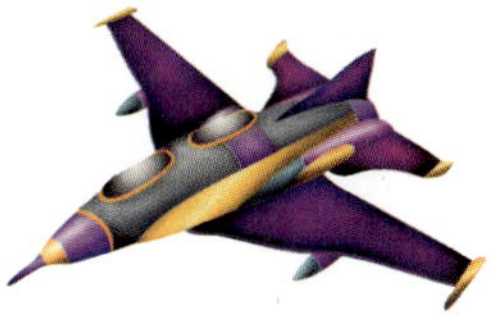

jet

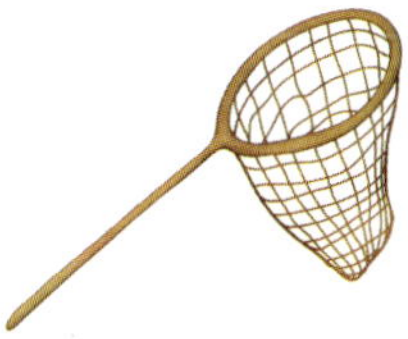

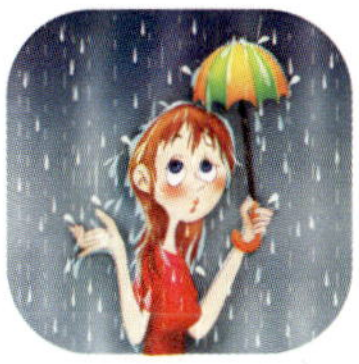

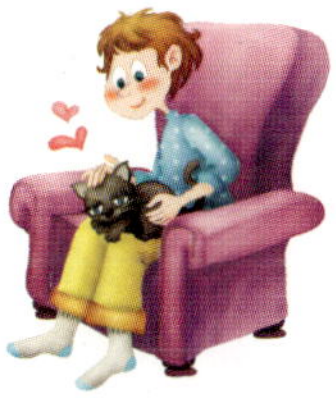

3. Learn

✏️ Match the words to the pictures.

wet •  • 

jet • • 

men • • 

🎧 **MP3 30** / Unit 5

Listen and circle the pictures that rhyme with "pen".

🎧 **MP3 31** / Unit 5

Listen and circle the pictures that rhyme with "pet".

 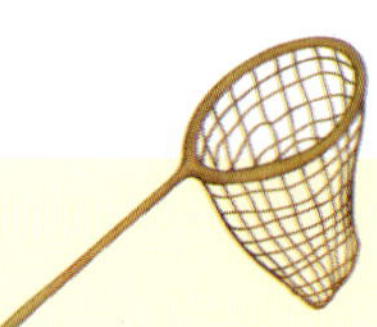  

Date　　.　　.　　.

4. Practice

 Listen and circle the correct pictures. 📄 **32** / Unit 5

1 

2 

3 

4 

✏️ Circle and write.

  en / et

h __________

  en / et

w __________

  en / et

n __________

 en / et

p __________

Listen and check ✔ the correct sentences. **MP3 33** / Unit 5

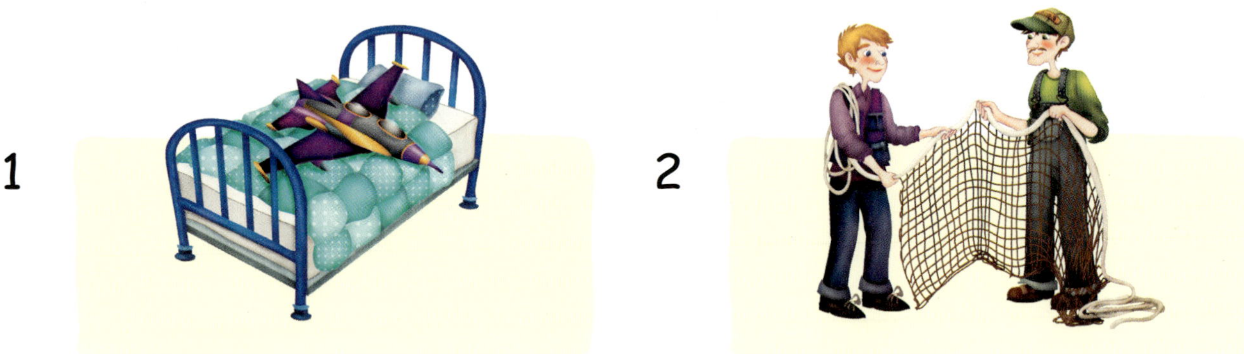

1

○ The jet is on the bed.
○ The pet is on the bed.

2

○ The hen has a net.
○ The men have a net.

3

○ The hen has a pen.
○ The ten has a pen.

4

○ The jet is wet.
○ The bed is wet.

Date   .   .   .

6. Homework

✏️ Write and circle the correct words.

n t m e n e t m e t

t e t e m e n t e n

e h e m p e n p e m

w t e w e w e t e w

Short vowel e

 **Listen and complete the words.** 🔊 **34** / Review 2

1  p •   • eg

2  b •   • en

3  n •   • ed

4  l •   • et

Short vowel e

✏️ Find the words. ↓ → ↘ ↑

red	wet	beg	ten	egg	men

t	i	d	k	m	p
u	e	r	l	f	s
b	g	n	e	g	g
n	e	g	h	d	t
e	b	w	e	t	v
m	a	c	j	n	o

Find these words on the picture and circle.

Rhyme time

 **Listen and repeat.**　.MP3 **35** / Review 2

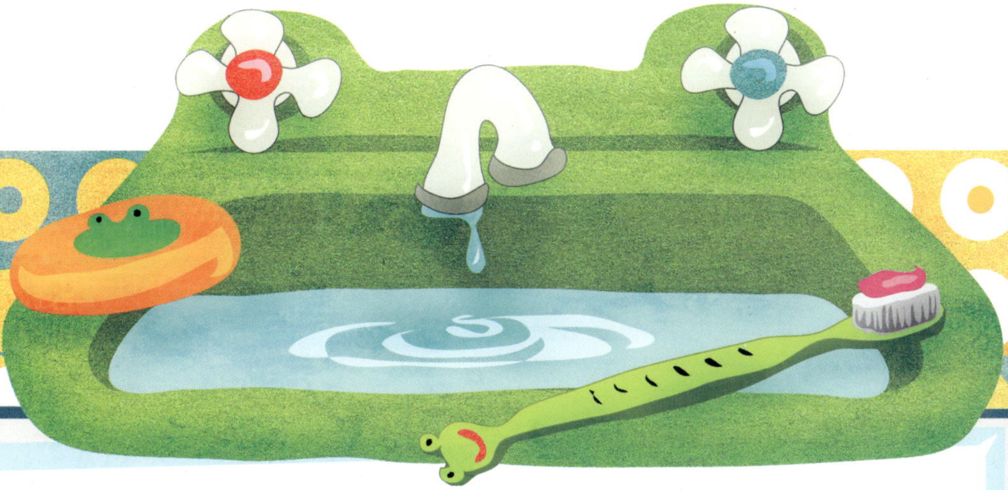

1. Ted is wed on a big red bed.

2. An egg with a leg begs for a peg.

3. A hen and ten men have a pen.

4. The jet and pet in the net are wet.

 **Listen and write the words.**  **36** / Review 2

1 _______________   6 _______________

2 _______________   7 _______________

3 _______________   8 _______________

4 _______________   9 _______________

5 _______________   10 _______________

10

Score _______________

Sight words

 Listen and write the sight words. **MP3** **37** / Review 2

1 we

2 the

3 he

4 eat

 Find the sight words. ↓ → ↘ ↑

| we | the | he | eat |

t	g	k	n	t
a	i	f	d	h
e	w	a	t	e
c	j	e	l	p
h	e	b	o	m

Short vowel i
-id   -ig

PP2-06
MP3

🎧 Listen and repeat. .MP3 **38** / Unit 6

i + d → id

hid

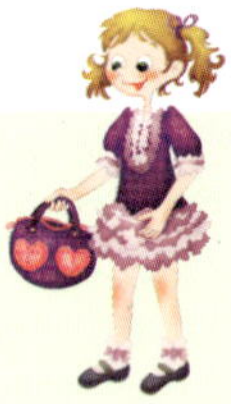

kid

lid

i + g → ig

big

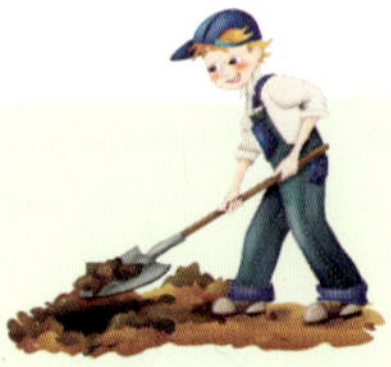

dig

pig

Date　　　．　　．　　．

2. Write

Listen, put on the stickers, and write. **MP3** **39** / Unit 6

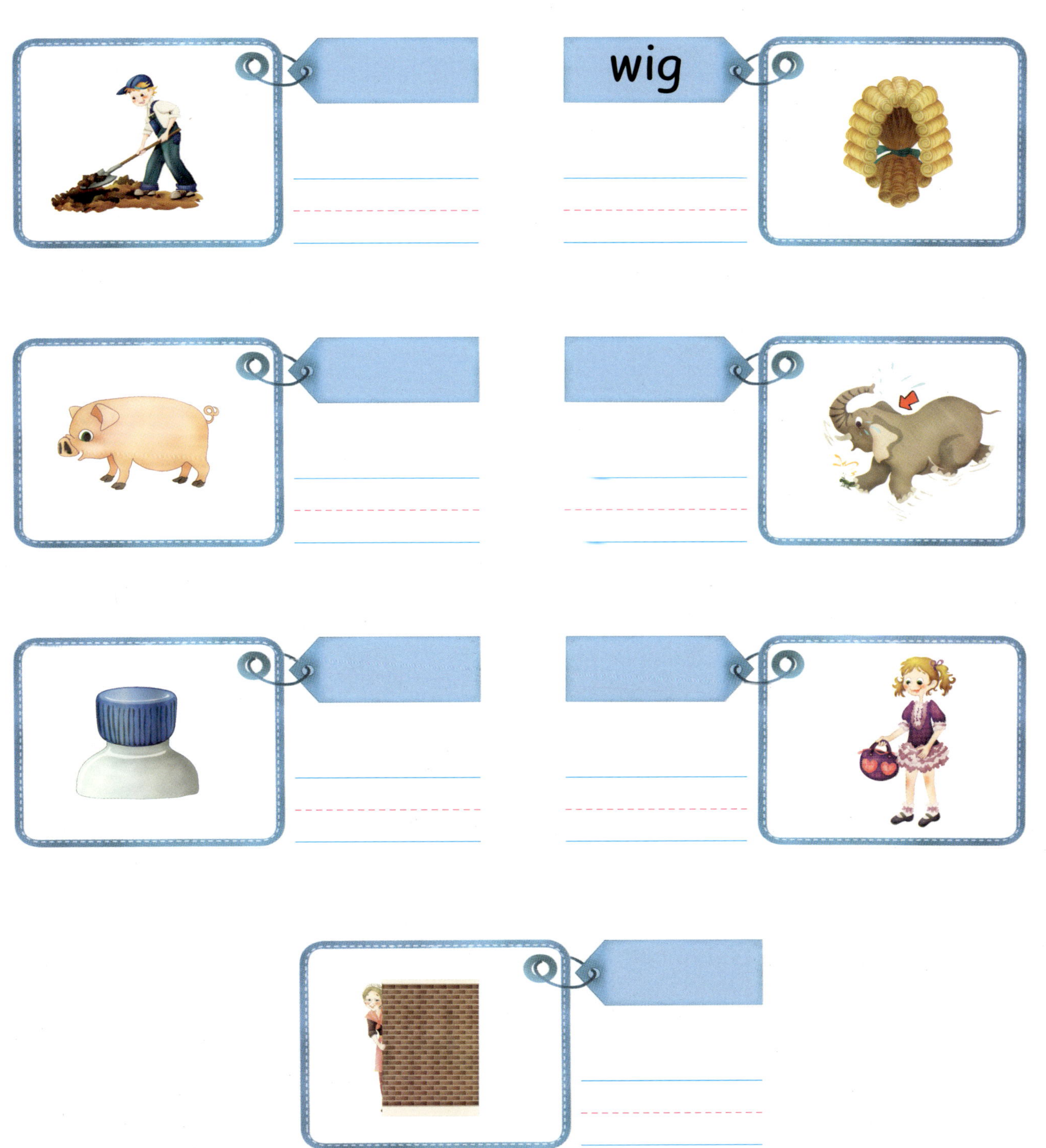

✏️ **Match the words to the pictures.**

kid •

wig •

lid •

📱 **40** / Unit 6

🎧 Listen and circle the pictures that rhyme with "pig".

📱 **41** / Unit 6

🎧 Listen and circle the pictures that rhyme with "hid".

Date . . .

4. Practice

Listen and circle the correct pictures. **.MP3** **42** / Unit 6

1

2

3

4

✏️ Circle and write.

id
ig

k_______

id
ig

l_______

id
ig

p_______

id
ig

b_______

Listen and check ✔ the correct sentences. **MP3** **43** / Unit 6

1

○ The kid has a wig.

○ The kid has a lid.

2

○ The pig has a wig.

○ The pig has a lid.

3

○ The wig is big.

○ The pig is big.

4

○ The wig is on the lid.

○ The pig is on the lid.

Date . . .

6. Homework

Unscramble the words and read.

g / i / p

i / k / d

i / g / w

d / i / l

g / b / i

d / g / i

i / h / d

Short vowel i
-in   -ip

1. Listen

PP2-07
MP3

🎧 Listen and repeat.  **44** / Unit 7

i + n → in

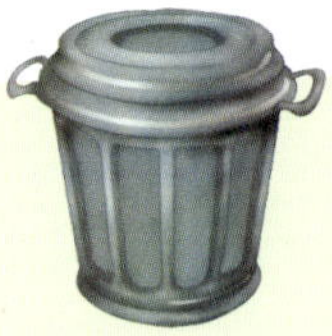

bin

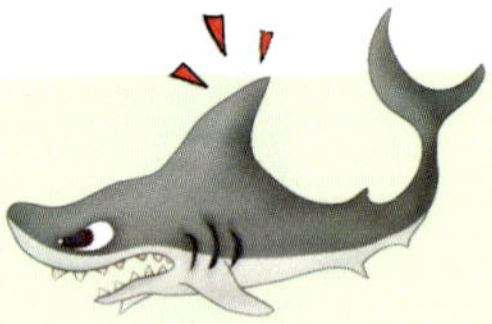

fin

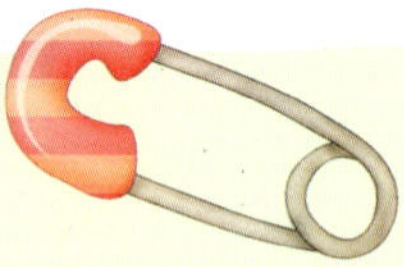

pin

i + p → ip

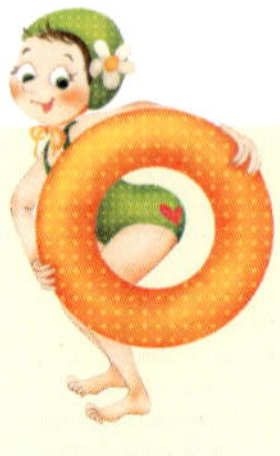

hip

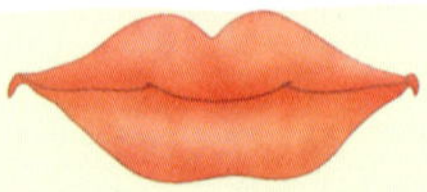

lip

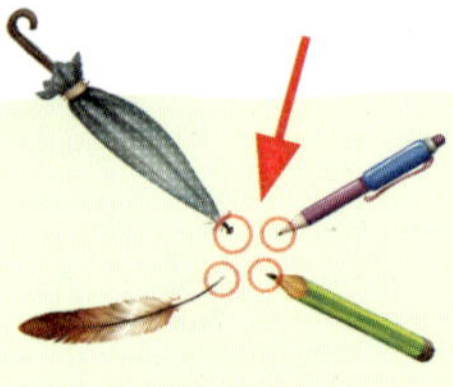

tip

Date ． ． ．

2. Write

 Listen, put on the stickers, and write. .MP3 **45** / Unit 7

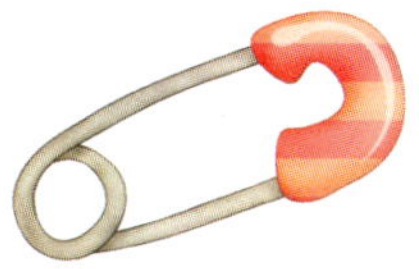

win

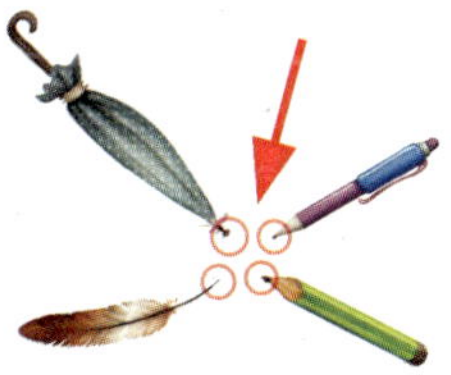

dip

Match the words to the pictures.

win ·

bin ·

dip ·

.MP3 46 / Unit 7

Listen and circle the pictures that rhyme with "pin".

.MP3 47 / Unit 7

Listen and circle the pictures that rhyme with "lip".

Date   .   .   .

4. Practice

🎧 Listen and circle the correct pictures. 📁 **48** / Unit 7

1 

2 

3 

4 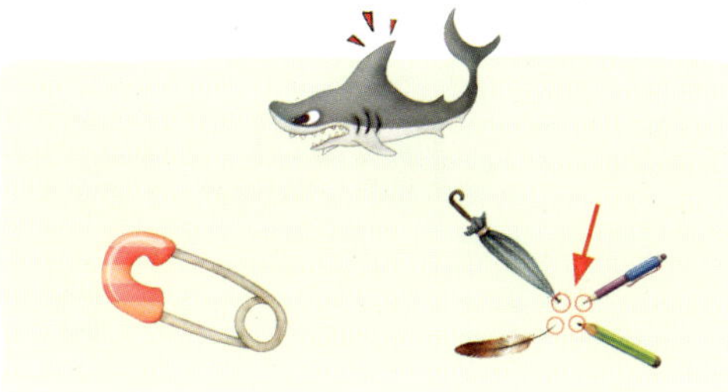

✏️ Circle and write.

b  ______

h ______

d ______

f ______

Listen and unscramble the words.
Then, match the words to the pictures. .MP3 **49** / Unit 7

1   i   n   p   •

p _______

2   p   i   d   •

_______ p

3   f   n   i   •

i _______

4   n   i   b   •

_______ n

5   i   p   t   •

t _______

Date . . .

6. Homework

 Write and circle the correct words.

f a n i f i n h f i

h e p i p h i p h p

w i h i w n i w i n

i l p l l p i l i p

Short vowel i
-it   -ix

Listen and repeat.  **50** / Unit 8

i + t → it

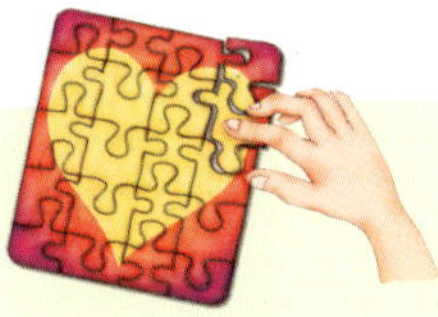

fit

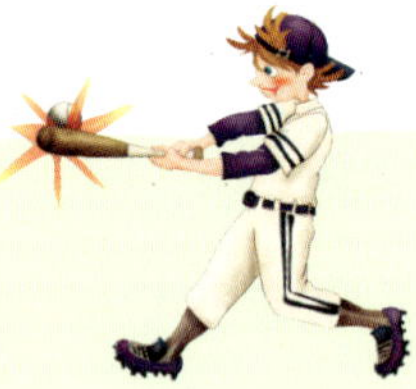

hit

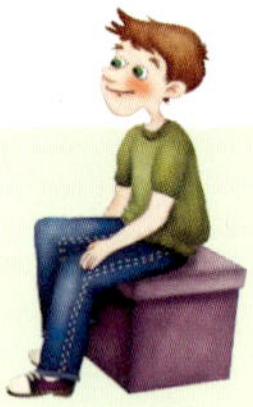

sit

i + x → ix

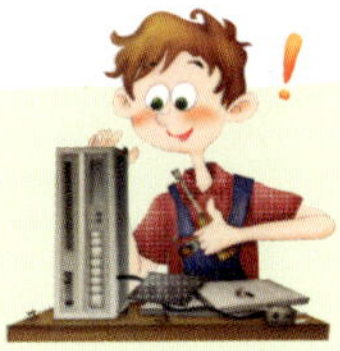

fix

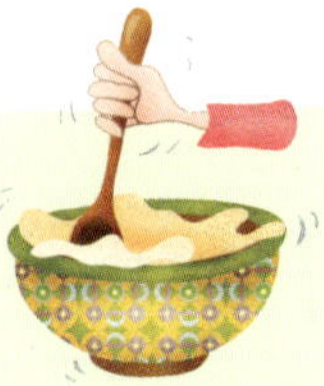

mix

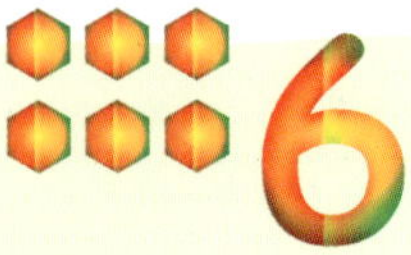

six

Date . . .

2. Write

Listen, put on the stickers, and write. MP3 51 / Unit 8

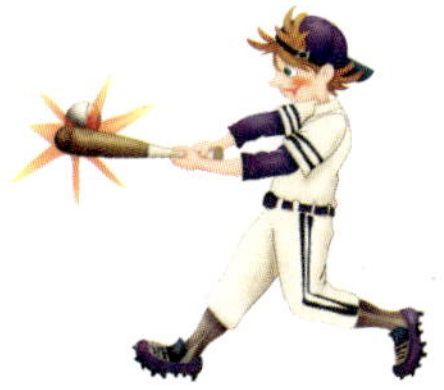

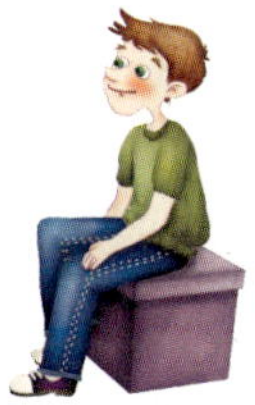

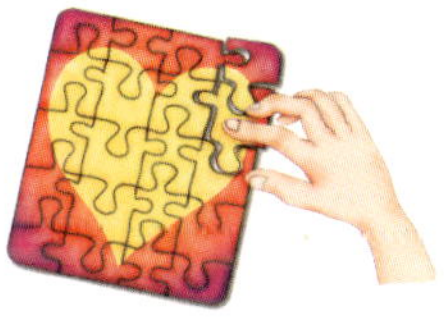

pit

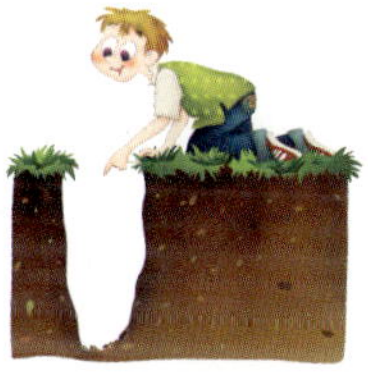

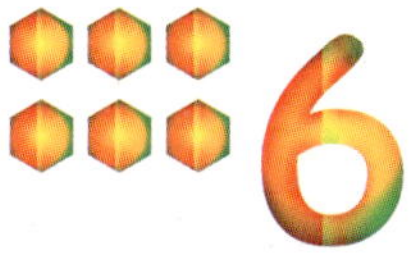

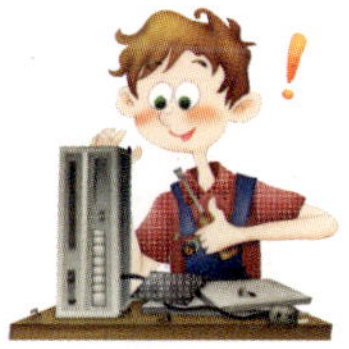

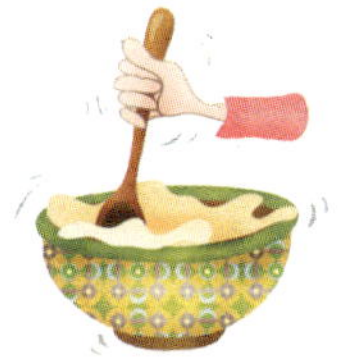

✏️ Match the words to the pictures.

fit   •

pit   •

six   •

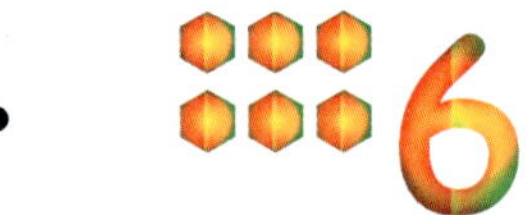

.MP3 **52** / Unit8

🎧 Listen and circle the pictures that rhyme with "fix".

.MP3 **53** / Unit8

🎧 Listen and circle the pictures that rhyme with "hit".

Date　　　.　　.　　.

4. Practice

Listen and circle the correct pictures. 🎧 **.MP3** **54** / Unit 8

1 

2 

3 

4 

✏️ Circle and write.

  it
 ix

f ______

  it
 ix

f ______

  it
 ix

s ______

  it
 ix

s ______

5. Activity

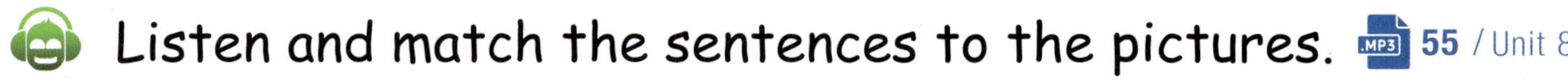

Listen and match the sentences to the pictures. 🎧 .MP3 **55** / Unit 8

1 The men sit on the box. •

2 The boy hits the ball. •

3 There are six pens. •

4 My hen is in a big pit. •

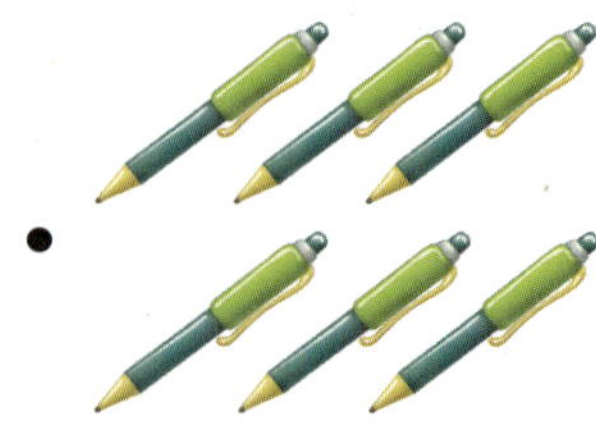

Date .   .   .

6. Homework

 Look and circle. Does the picture have a "short i" sound?

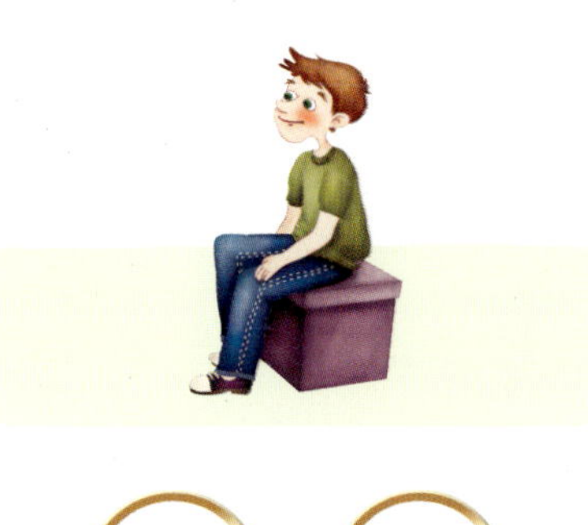

O   X

O   X

O   X

O   X

O   X

O   X

O   X

O   X

O   X

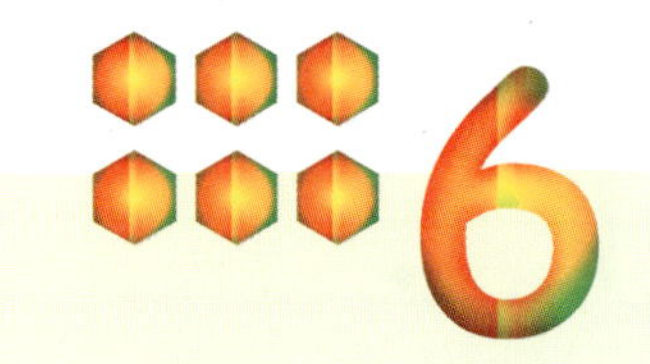

O   X

O   X

O   X

Short vowel i

PP2-R-3
MP3

Listen and complete the words. MP3 **56** / Review 3

1      h ·   · id

2      l ·   · in

3   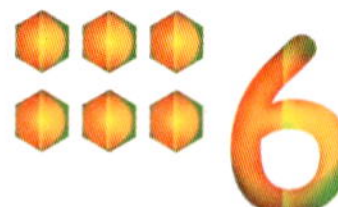   s ·   · it

4      p ·   · ix

5      k ·   · ip

6   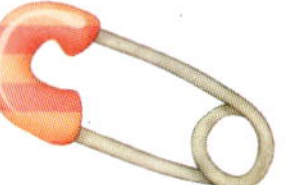   p ·   · ig

Short vowel i

✏️ **Find the words.** ↓ → ↘ ↑

sit   lid   mix   big   win   hip

g	a	e	p	n	o
i	b	w	i	n	u
b	s	c	l	i	d
d	i	h	m	e	g
f	t	i	j	i	k
l	m	p	n	o	x

Find these words on the picture and circle.

Rhyme time

Listen and repeat. MP3 57 / Review 3

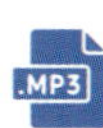

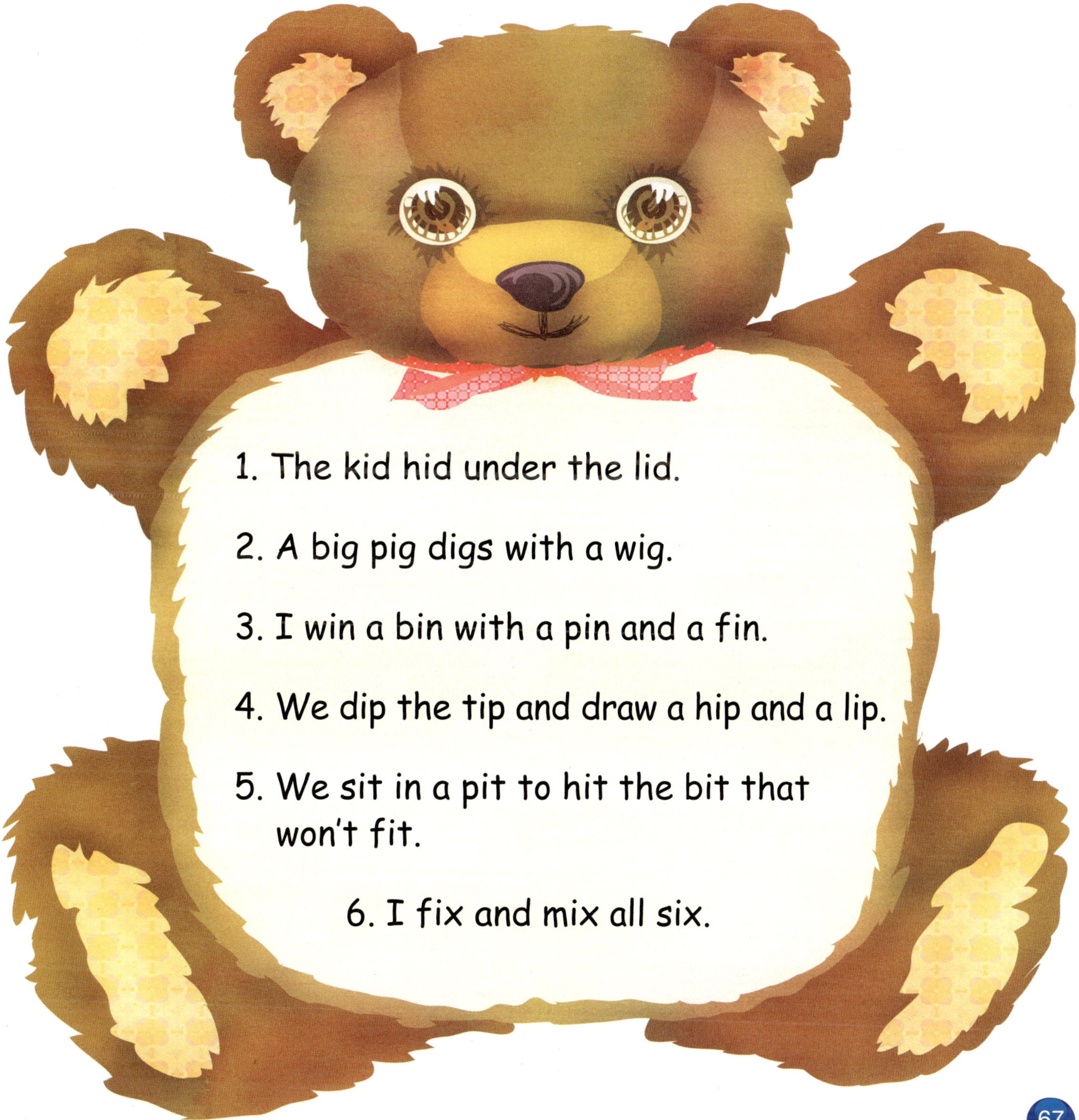

1. The kid hid under the lid.
2. A big pig digs with a wig.
3. I win a bin with a pin and a fin.
4. We dip the tip and draw a hip and a lip.
5. We sit in a pit to hit the bit that won't fit.
6. I fix and mix all six.

 Listen and write the words.  **58** / Review 3

1 ________________   6 ________________

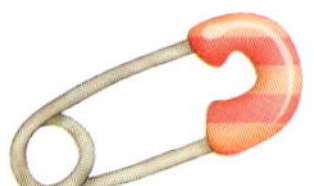

2 ________________   7 ________________

3 ________________   8 ________________

4 ________________   9 ________________

5 ________________   10 ________________

Score ________________

 **Listen and write the sight words.** MP3 **59** / Review 3

1 it

2 is

3 will

4 with

✏️ Find the sight words. ↓ → ↘ ↑

it

is

will

with

a	w	i	l	l
k	m	h	n	d
f	r	t	i	o
i	b	i	t	g
h	s	w	c	j

Short vowel o
-og -op

1. Listen

PP2-09
MP3

Listen and repeat.  **60** / Unit 9

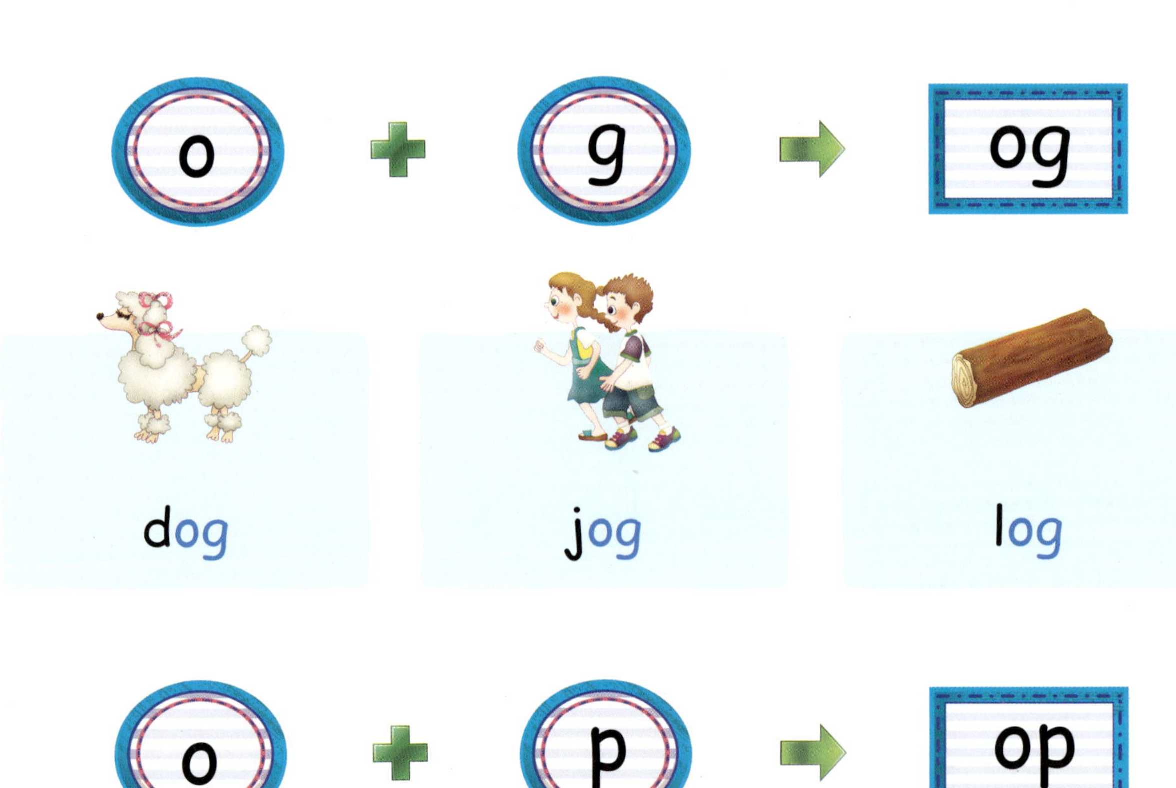

Date ___ . ___ . ___

2. Write

🎧 **Listen, put on the stickers, and write.** MP3 **61** / Unit 9

fog

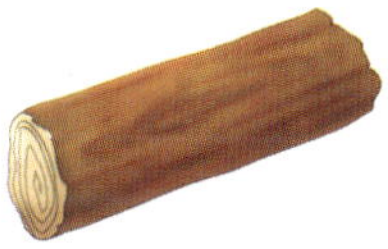

pop

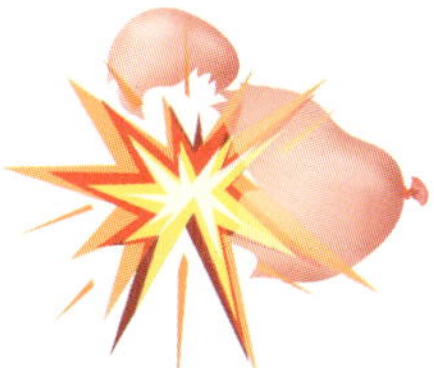

3. Learn

✏️ **Match the words to the pictures.**

cop • • 

jog • •

log • •

🎧 **62** / Unit 9

Listen and circle the pictures that rhyme with "top".

🎧 **63** / Unit 9

Listen and circle the pictures that rhyme with "log".

Date　　　.　　.　　.

4. Practice

Listen and circle the correct pictures.　**64** / Unit 9

1 

2 

3 

4

Circle and write.

og
op

t＿＿＿＿＿＿

og
op

d＿＿＿＿＿＿

og
op

f＿＿＿＿＿＿

og
op

j＿＿＿＿＿＿

Find and circle the words.

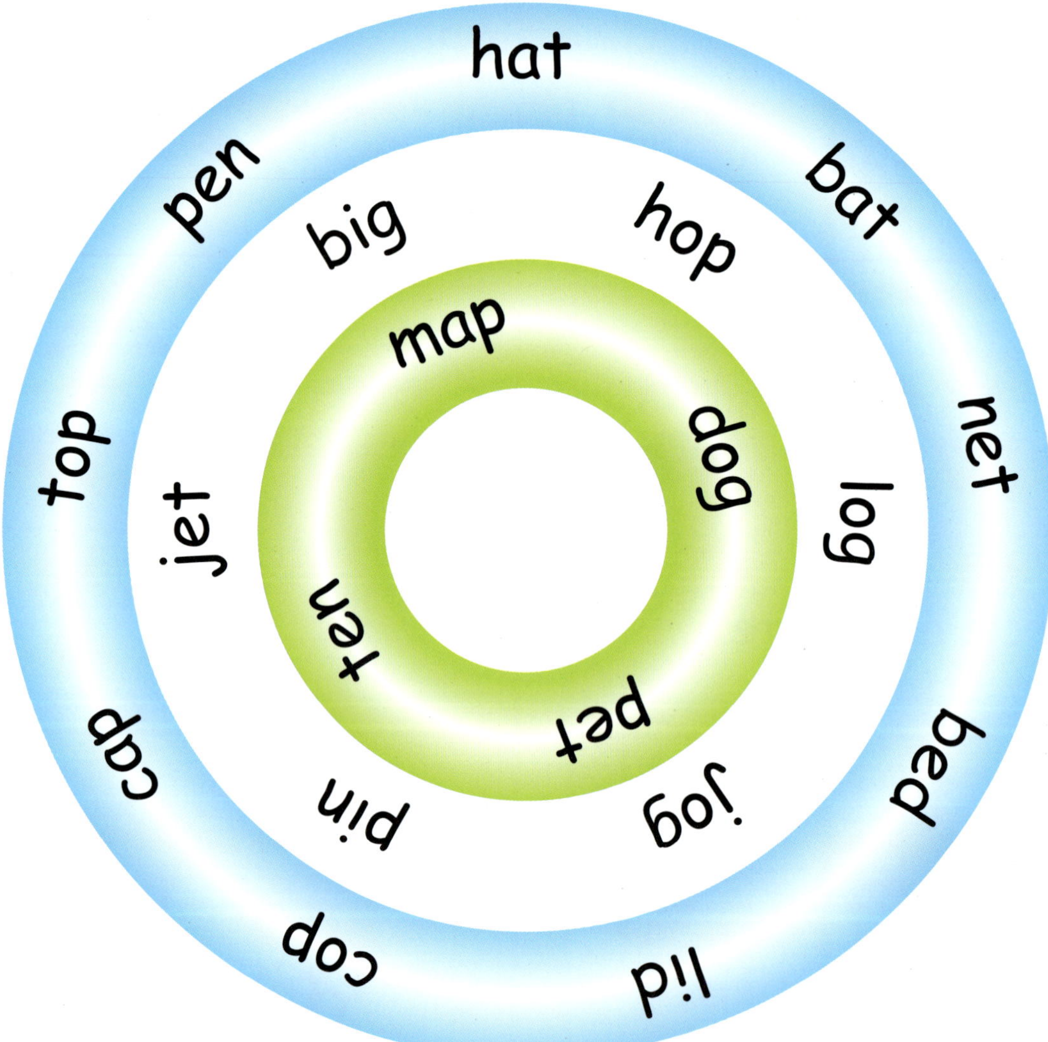

dog   cop   top   hop   log   jog

Date . . .

6. Homework

✏️ Unscramble the words and read.

Short vowel o

-ot   -ox

PP2-10
MP3

 Listen and repeat. 65 / Unit 10

o + t → ot

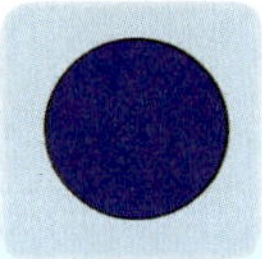

dot

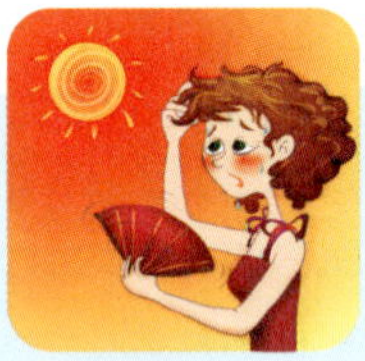

hot

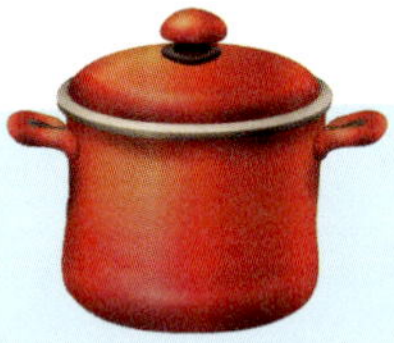

pot

o + x → ox

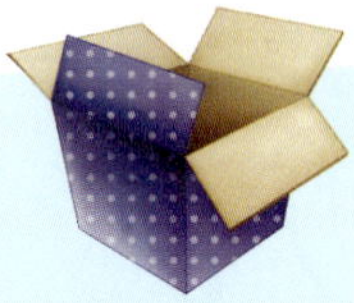

box

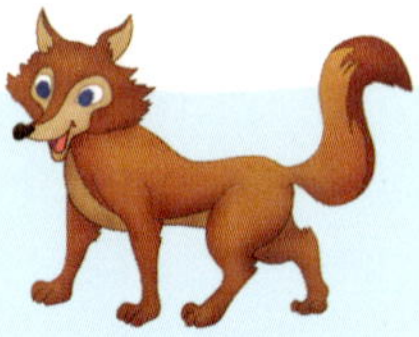

fox

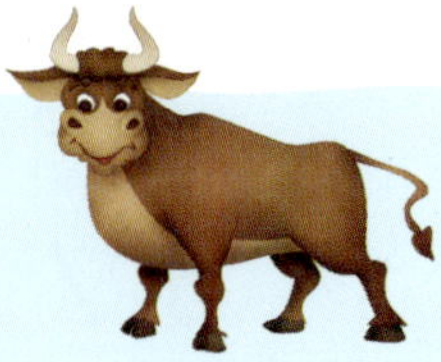

ox

Date . . .

2. Write

🎧 Listen, put on the stickers, and write. **66** / Unit 10

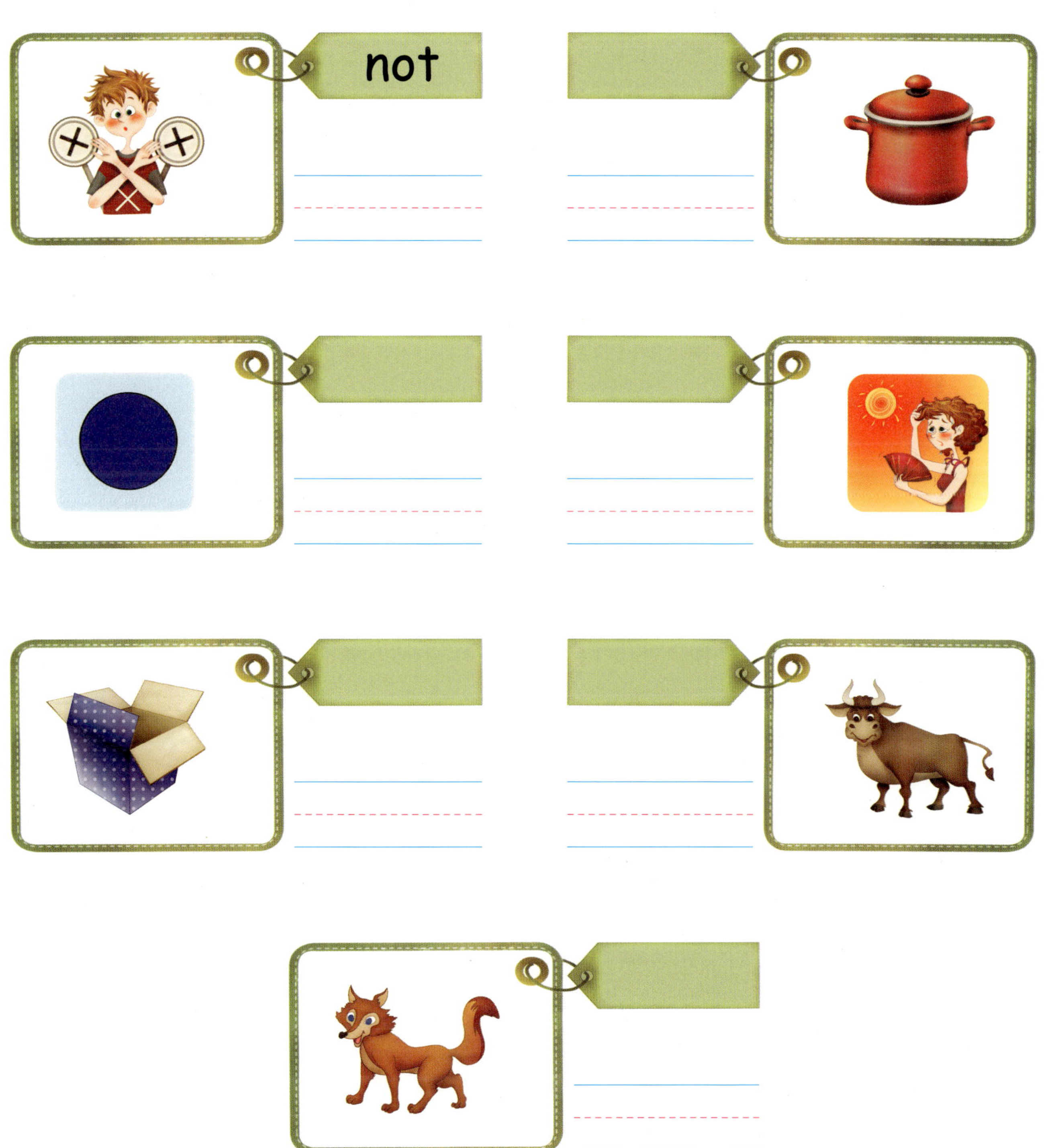

✏️ Match the words to the pictures.

box •   • 

pot •   • 

dot •   • 

🎧 **MP3** **67** / Unit 10

🎧 Listen and circle the pictures that rhyme with "dot".

🎧 **MP3** **68** / Unit 10

🎧 Listen and circle the pictures that rhyme with "ox".

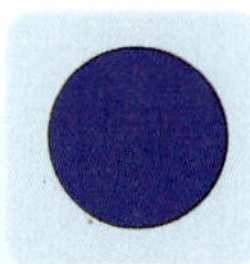  

Date   .   .   .

4. Practice

Listen and circle the correct pictures. MP3 **69** / Unit 10

1

2

3

4

Circle and write.

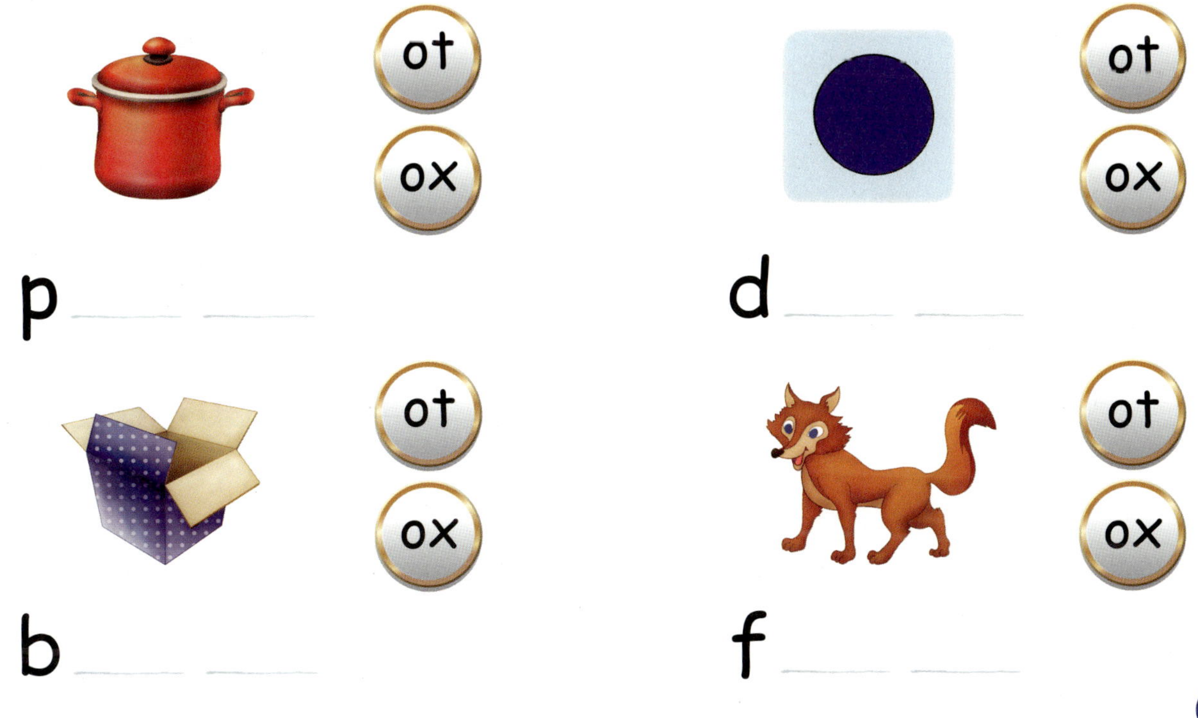

ot
ox

p _______

ot
ox

d _______

ot
ox

b _______

ot
ox

f _______

 Listen and check ✔ the correct sentences.  **70** / Unit 10

1

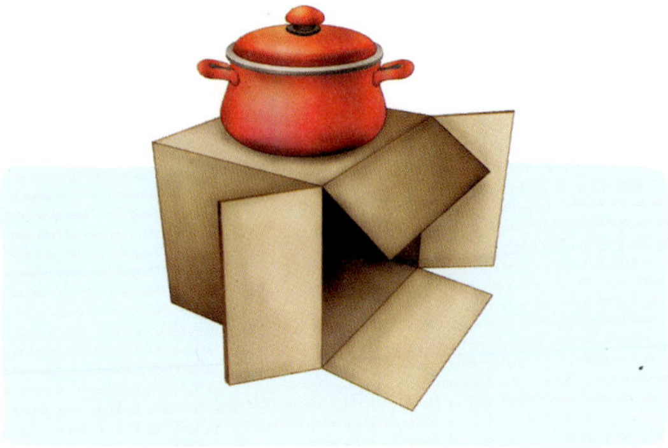

◯ The box has a dot.

◯ The hot pot has a dot.

2

◯ The pot is on the box.

◯ The dot is on the ox.

3

◯ The ox has a pot.

◯ The fox has a pot.

4

◯ The dog hops over the ox.

◯ The dog hops over the box.

6. Homework

Look and circle. Does the picture have a "short o" sound?

Short vowel o

PP2-R-4
MP3

🎧 **Listen and complete the words.** 🎵 **71** / Review 4

1  h •   • ox

2  d •   • ot

3  f •   • op

4  t •   • og

Short vowel o

✏️ Find the words. ↓ → ↘ ↑

jog   not   hop   fog   box   pot

a	e	b	o	x	c
h	i	b	j	d	h
c	j	o	g	m	o
g	l	n	p	r	p
o	n	f	o	o	s
f	p	g	k	t	t

Find these words on the picture and circle.

Rhyme time

Listen and repeat. MP3 **72** / Review 4

1. A dog with a log can jog in the fog.

2. The ball might pop when a cop hops on top.

3. The pot is not hot near the dot.

4. A fox and an ox sit in a box.

 Listen and write the words. MP3 **73** / Review 4

1 _______________ 6 _______________

2 _______________ 7 _______________

3 _______________ 8 _______________

4 _______________ 9 _______________

5 _______________ 10 _______________

Score _______________

Sight words

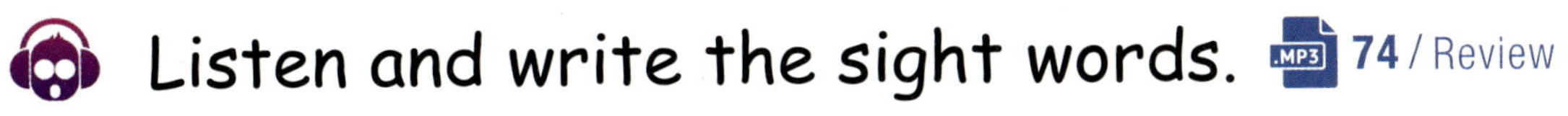 Listen and write the sight words. .MP3 **74** / Review 4

1 **to**

2 **on**

3 **off**

4 **do**

✏ Find the sight words. ↓ → ↘ ↑

to
on
off
do

v	i	r	w	g
o	y	u	k	o
s	f	j	a	d
h	m	f	o	n
z	x	t	o	p

Short vowel u

-ug   -un

 Listen and repeat. 75 / Unit 11

u + g → ug

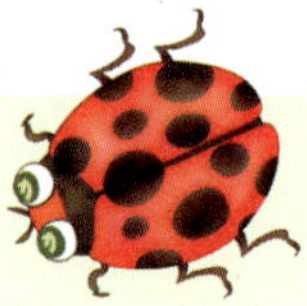

bug

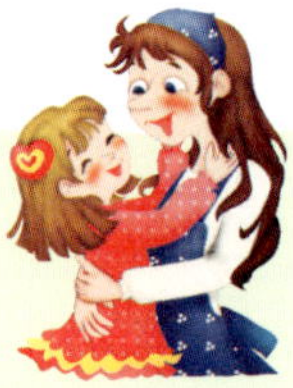

hug

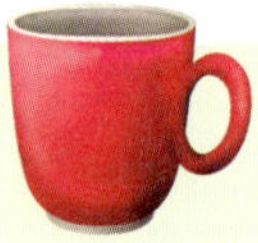

mug

u + n → un

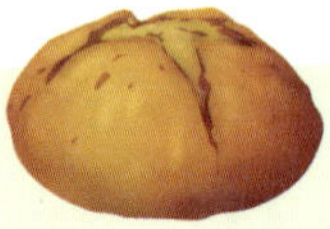

bun

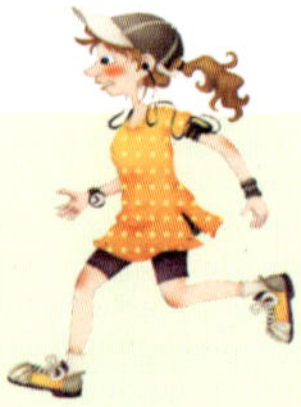

run

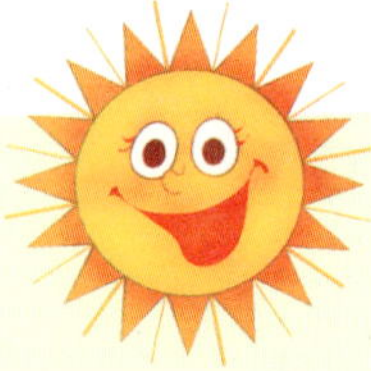

sun

Date . . .

2. Write

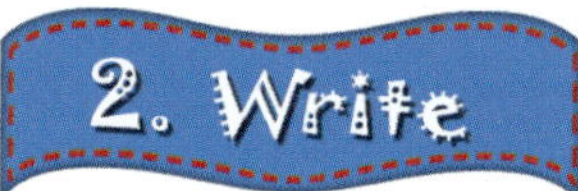

Listen, put on the stickers, and write. MP3 76 / Unit 11

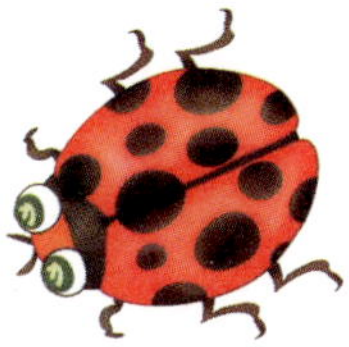

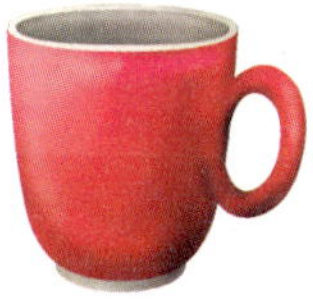

rug

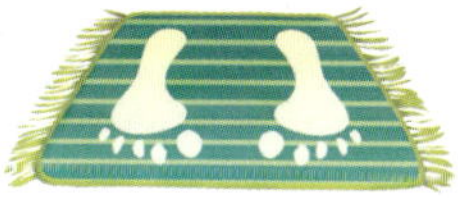

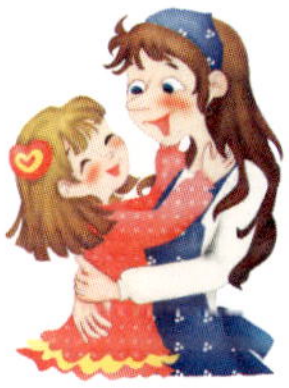

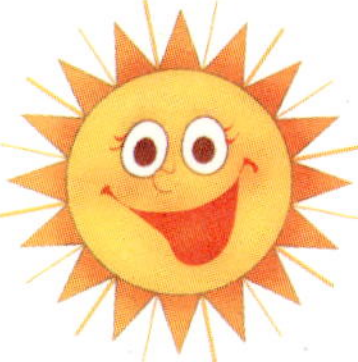

gun

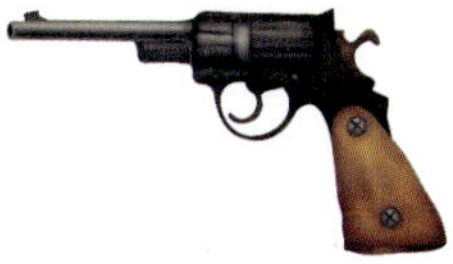

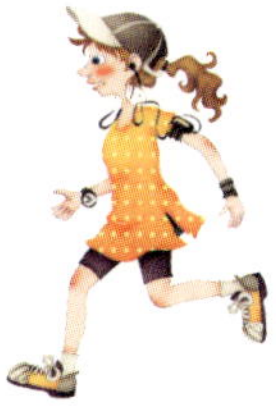

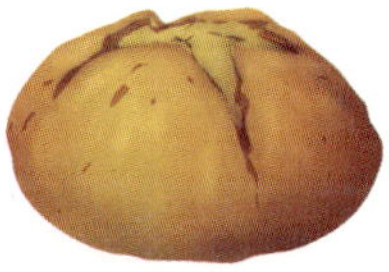

 Match the words to the pictures.

bun •

rug •

gun •

.MP3 **77** / Unit 11

Listen and circle the pictures that rhyme with "gun".

.MP3 **78** / Unit 11

Listen and circle the pictures that rhyme with "hug".

Date . . .

4. Practice

Listen and circle the correct pictures. **MP3** **79** / Unit 11

1 

2 

3 

4 

Circle and write.

  ug  un

r ______

  ug  un

h ______

  ug un

b ______

  ug  un

r ______

5. Activity

Write the letter in the puzzle.

Complete the words and read.
Then, circle the correct pictures.

m ___ g

s ___ n

g ___ n

r ___ g

Date　　.　　.　　.

6. Homework

 Circle the correct words and read the sentences.

A man has a **mug** / **rug**.

A cat hugs the **bun** / **bug**.

A bug is on the **gun** / **rug**.

The **sun** / **bun** sets.

Short vowel u

-up   -ut

PP2-12
MP3

Listen and repeat. **80** / Unit 12

u + p → up

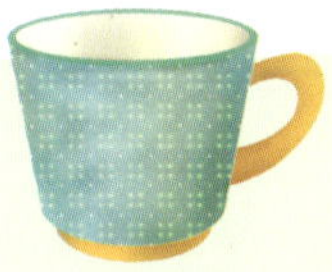

cup

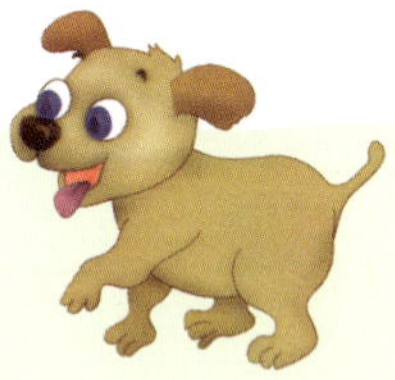

pup

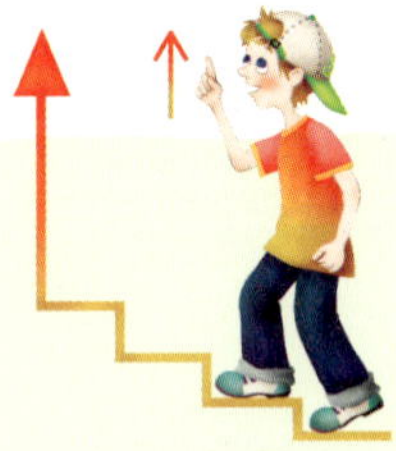

up

u + t → ut

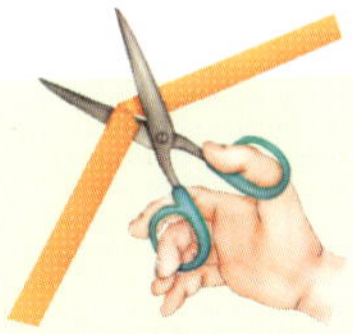

cut

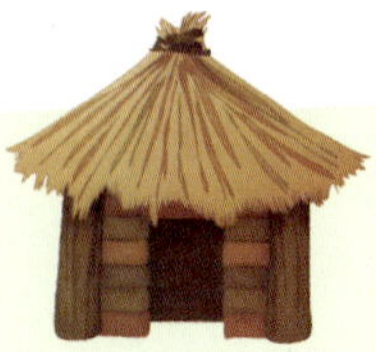

hut

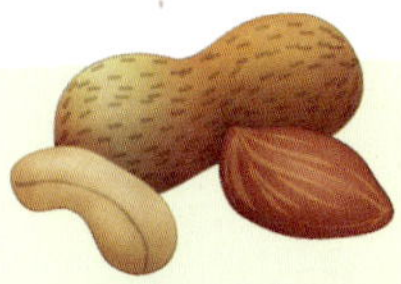

nut

Date　　　.　　.　　.

2. Write

Listen, put on the stickers, and write. **.MP3** **81** / Unit 12

✏️ **Match the words to the pictures.**

cut •

pup •

hut •

• 

• 

• 

📄 **82** / Unit 12

🎧 **Listen and circle the pictures that rhyme with "cup".**

📄 **83** / Unit 12

🎧 **Listen and circle the pictures that rhyme with "hut".**

  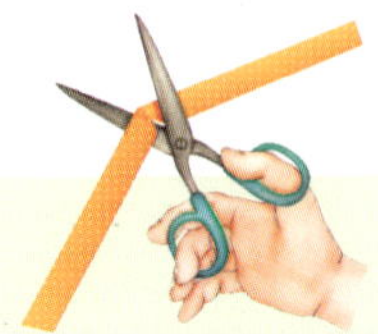 

Date _______ . _____ . _____

4. Practice

🎧 Listen and circle the correct pictures. **84** / Unit 12

1 

2 

3 

4 

✏️ Circle and write.

  up  ut

c _______

  up  ut

p _______

 up ut

c _______

  up ut

n _______

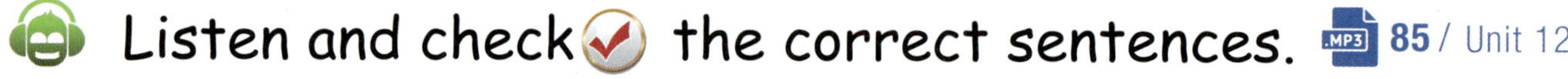

Listen and check ✔ the correct sentences. **MP3** **85** / Unit 12

1

◯ The bug hugs the nut.   ◯ The bug is on the hut.

◯ The bug hugs the cup.   ◯ The nut is on the hut.

2

3

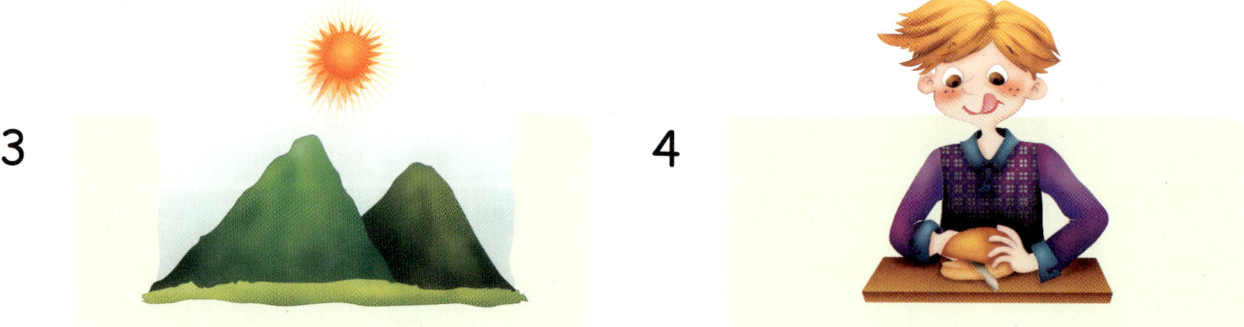

◯ The hut is up.   ◯ The kid cuts the nut.

◯ The sun is up.   ◯ The kid cuts the bun.

4

Date   .   .

6. Homework

Write and circle the correct words.

n t u h u t n u t n

c u c u p u p c u c

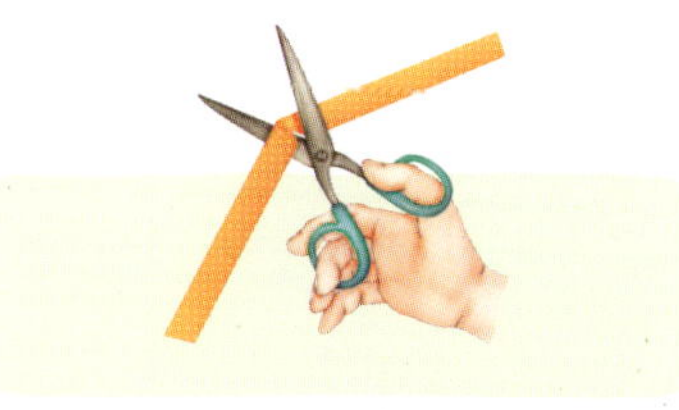

c t u c u c u t u c

u p u p b p b p u b

Short vowel u

 Listen and complete the words. **86** / Review 5

1  s •   • ug

2  c •   • up

3  b •   • un

4  c •   • ut

Short vowel u

✏️ **Find the words.** ↓ → ↘ ↑

pup   mug   gun   hut   run   hug

v	a	i	h	b	c
f	g	e	f	u	s
k	i	p	m	u	g
t	l	u	h	j	u
u	d	p	n	o	n
h	m	r	u	n	p

✏️ **Find these words on the picture and circle.**

 **Listen and repeat.** **87** / Review 5

 Listen and write the words. **88** / Review 5

1 ______________   6 ______________

2 ______________   7 ______________

3 ______________   8 ______________

4 ______________   9 ______________

5 ______________   10 ______________

Score ______________

Sight words

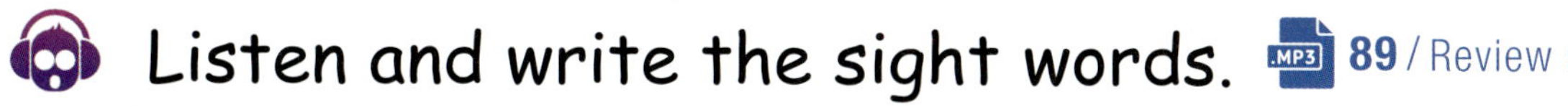

🎧 **Listen and write the sight words.** .MP3 **89** / Review 5

1 **out**

2 **us**

3 **our**

4 **under**

✏️ **Find the sight words.** ↓ → ↘ ↑

out	under
us	
our	

z	a	c	k	l
o	o	p	t	s
u	b	u	d	u
r	e	i	t	o
u	n	d	e	r

Memo

Memo

Unit 1	sad	bag	bad	wag	dad	tag
Unit 2	jam	pan	ram	fan	can	ham
Unit 3	mat	cap	cat	map	hat	tap
Unit 4	beg	Ted	red	bed	peg	leg
Unit 5	net	pen	ten	pet	wet	hen
Unit 6	big	hid	kid	dig	lid	pig
Unit 7	tip	fin	lip	pin	bin	hip
Unit 8	fit	hit	six	sit	mix	fix
Unit 9	cop	dog	log	hop	top	jog
Unit 10	dot	ox	fox	box	hot	pot
Unit 11	sun	bun	bug	run	hug	mug
Unit 12	cup	cut	up	pup	hut	nut

Phonics PARTY

Short Vowel Sounds

Workbook

2

WorldCom Edu

Phonics PARTY 2

Workbook

UNIT 1

-ad -ag

A Choose and write.

d b m s

+

ad

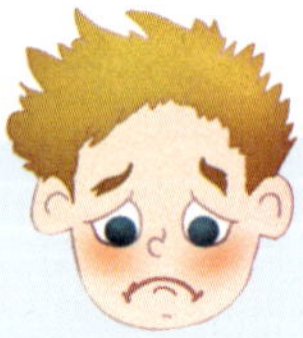

sad

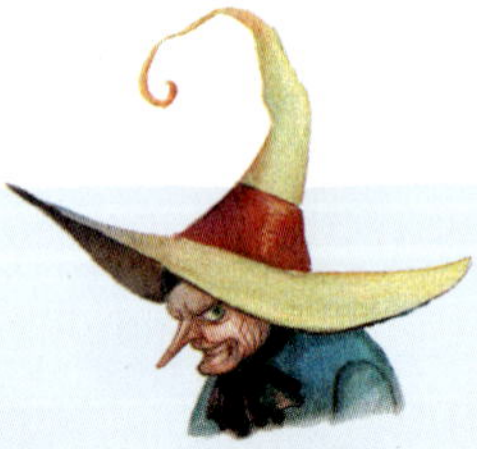

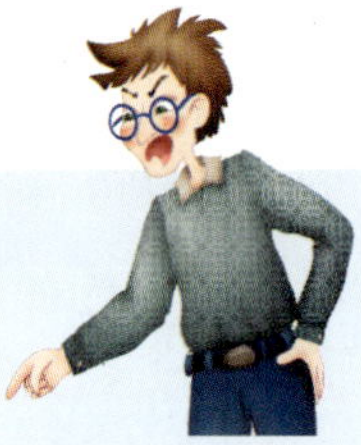

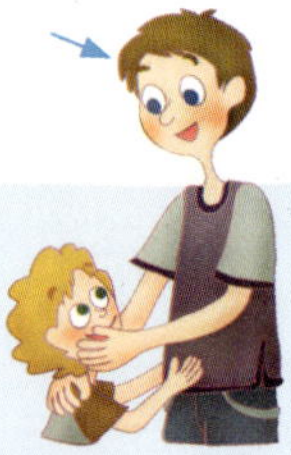

  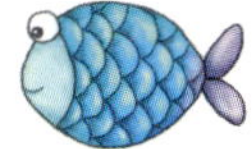    

B Choose and write.

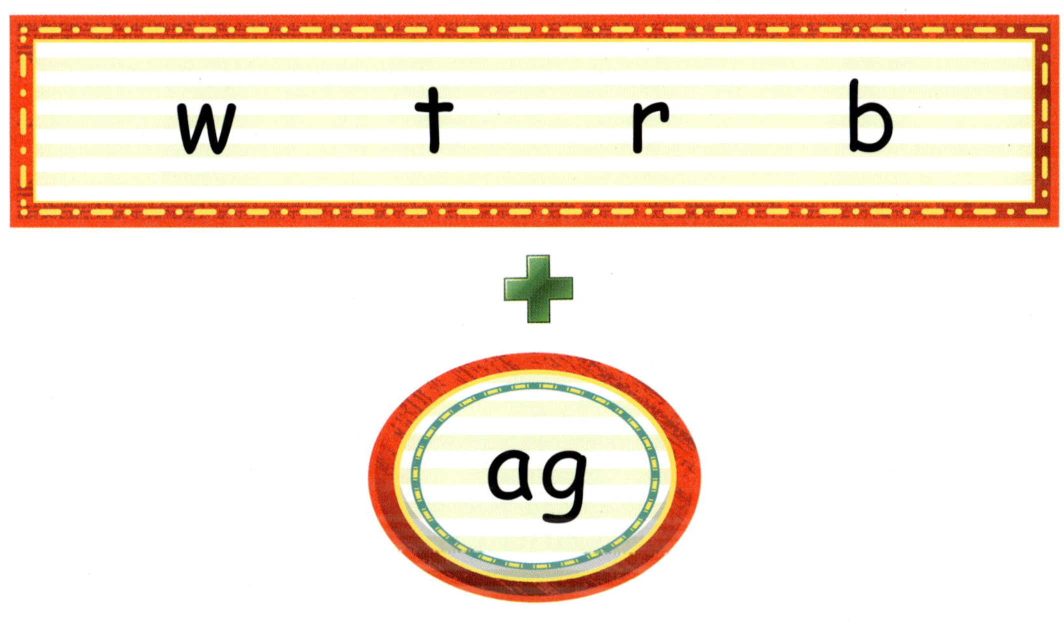

C Circle the correct words.

1   sad   (dad)

2   mad   bad

3   wag   tag

4   rag   bag

D Circle the correct word and color the picture.

He is (sad) / mad.

This is a tag / bag.

E Complete the words.

w**ag**

b ______

s ______

r ______

b ______

m ______

t ______

d ______

-am   -an

 Choose and write.

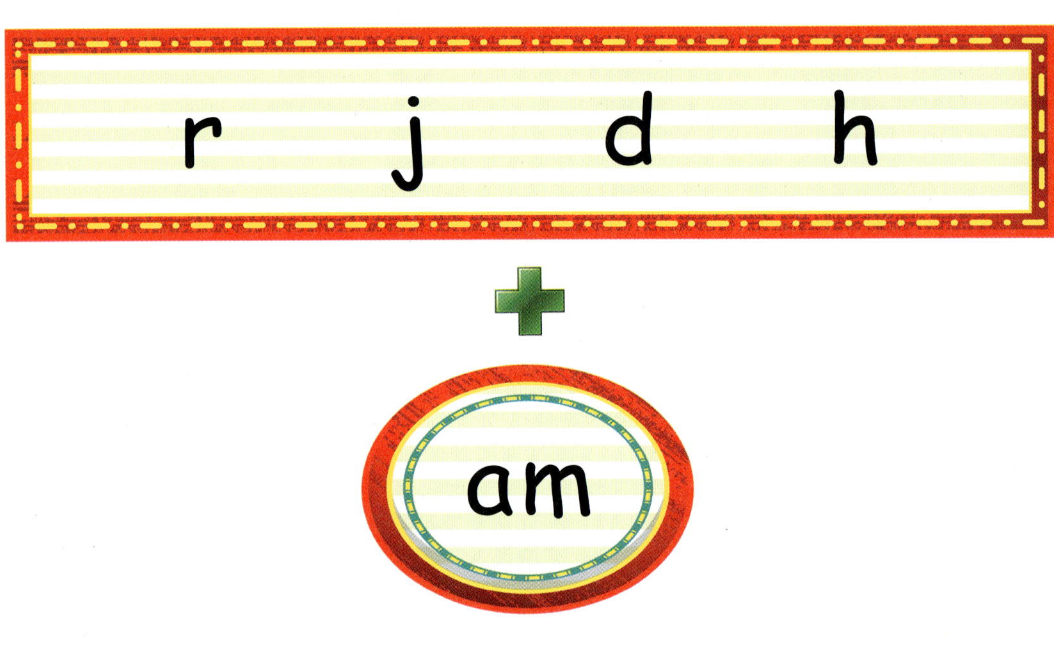

____

____

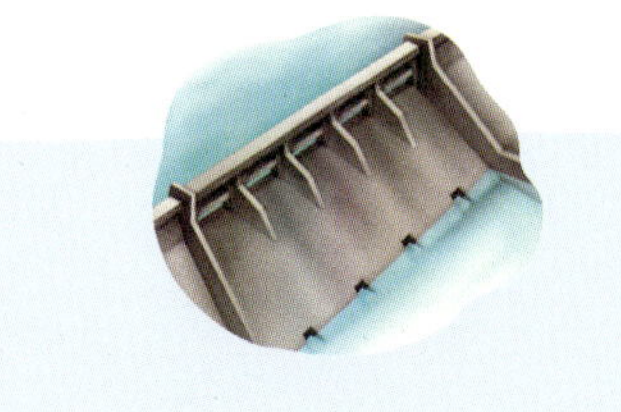

____

____

B **Choose and write.**

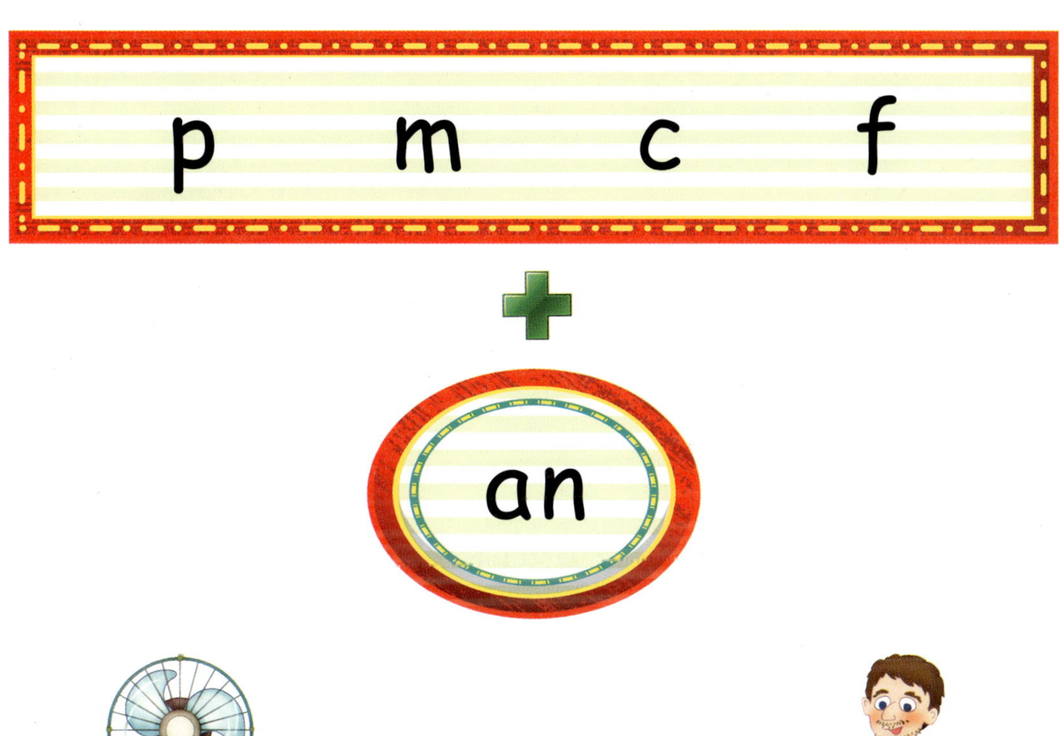

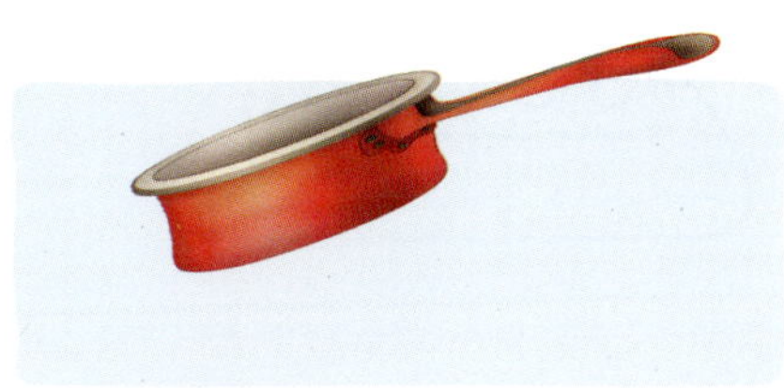

C **Circle the correct words.**

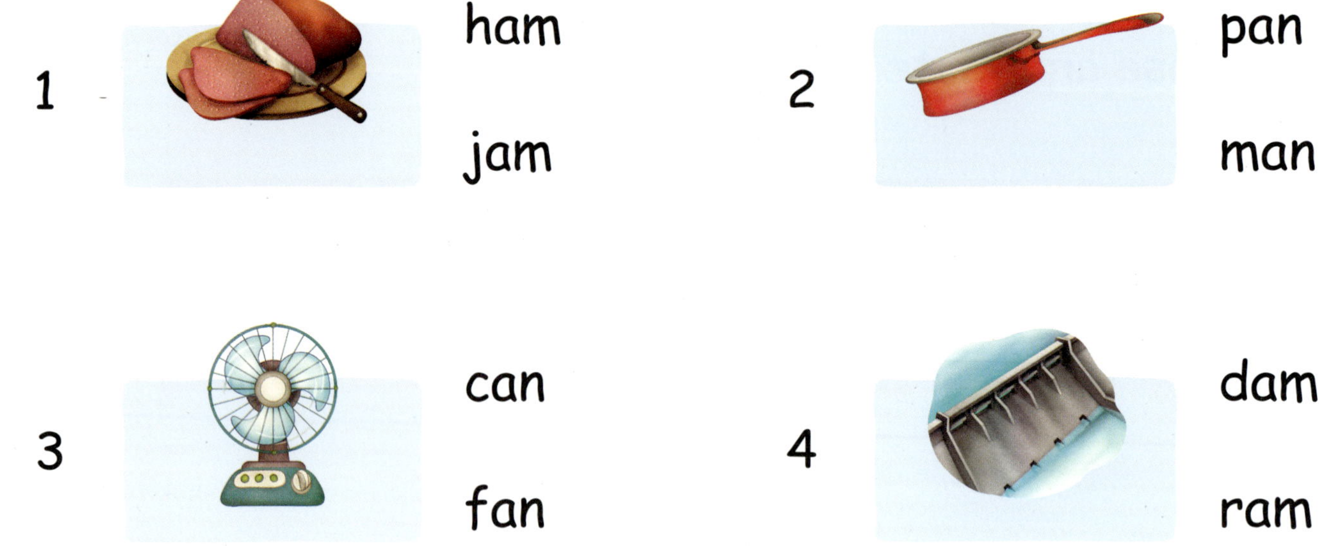

1. ham / jam

2. pan / man

3. can / fan

4. dam / ram

D **Circle the correct word and color the picture.**

This is a ram / jam.

This is a can / fan.

E Complete the words.

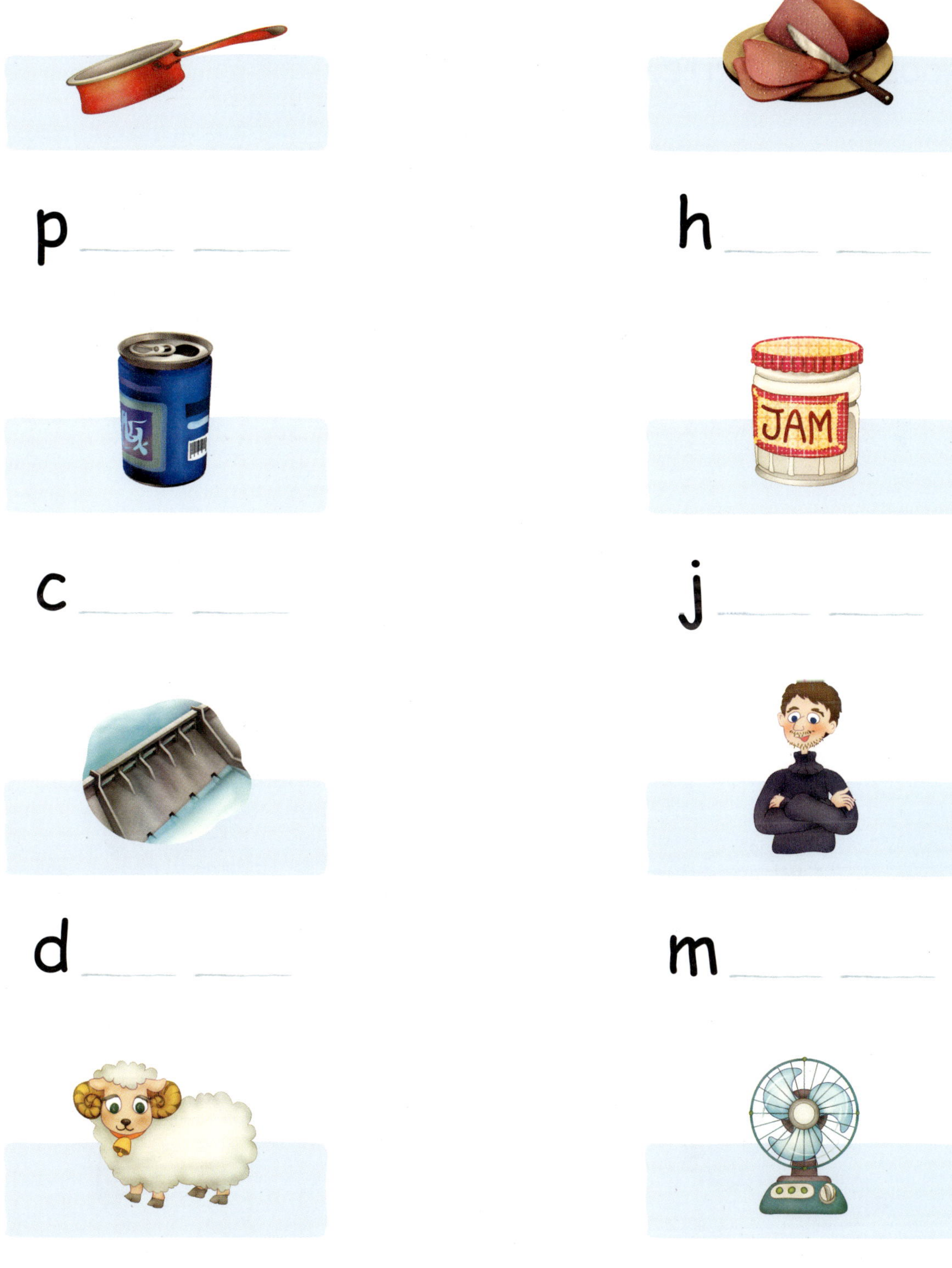

-ap   -at

A Choose and write.

  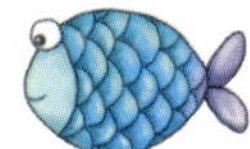    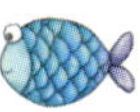

B Choose and write.

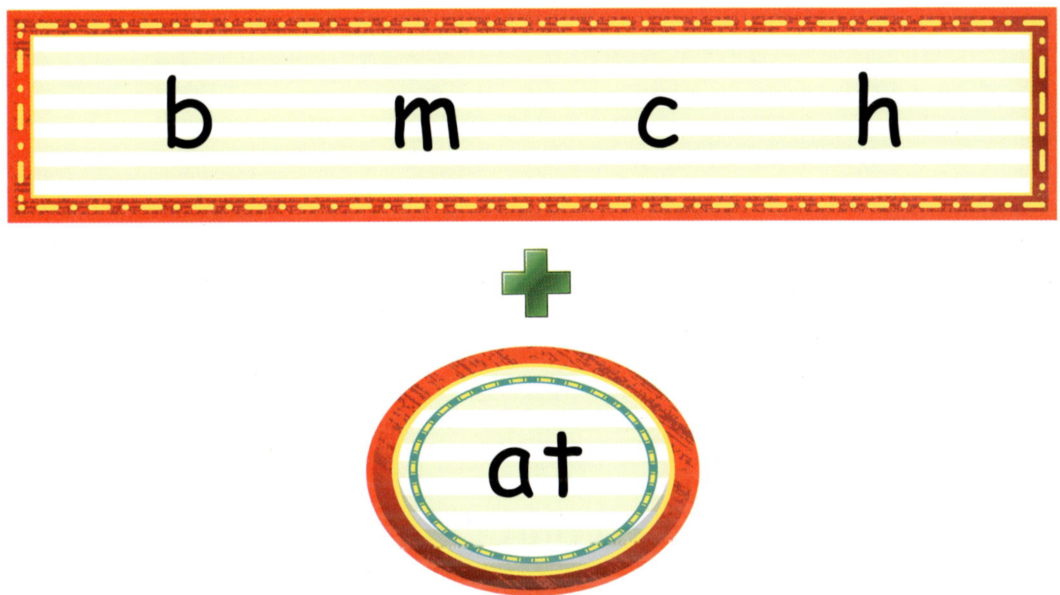

Circle the correct words.

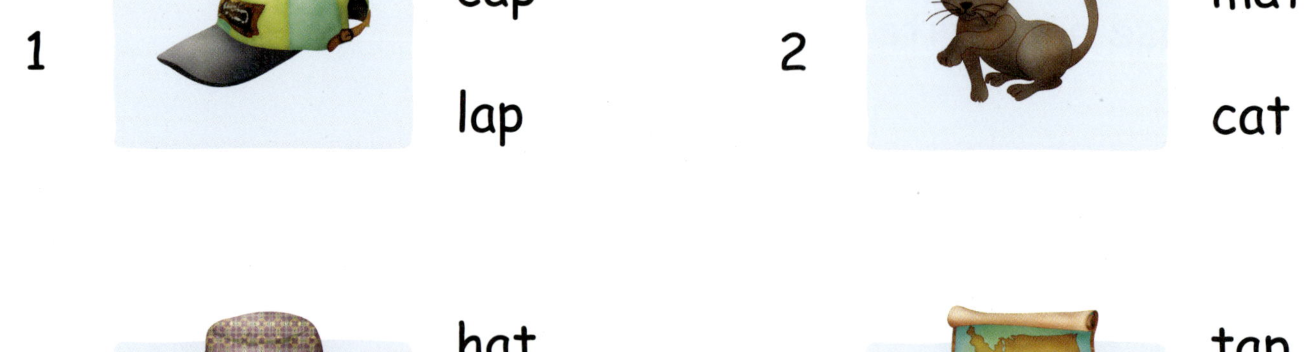

1 cap / lap

2 mat / cat

3 hat / bat

4 tap / map

Circle the correct word and color the picture.

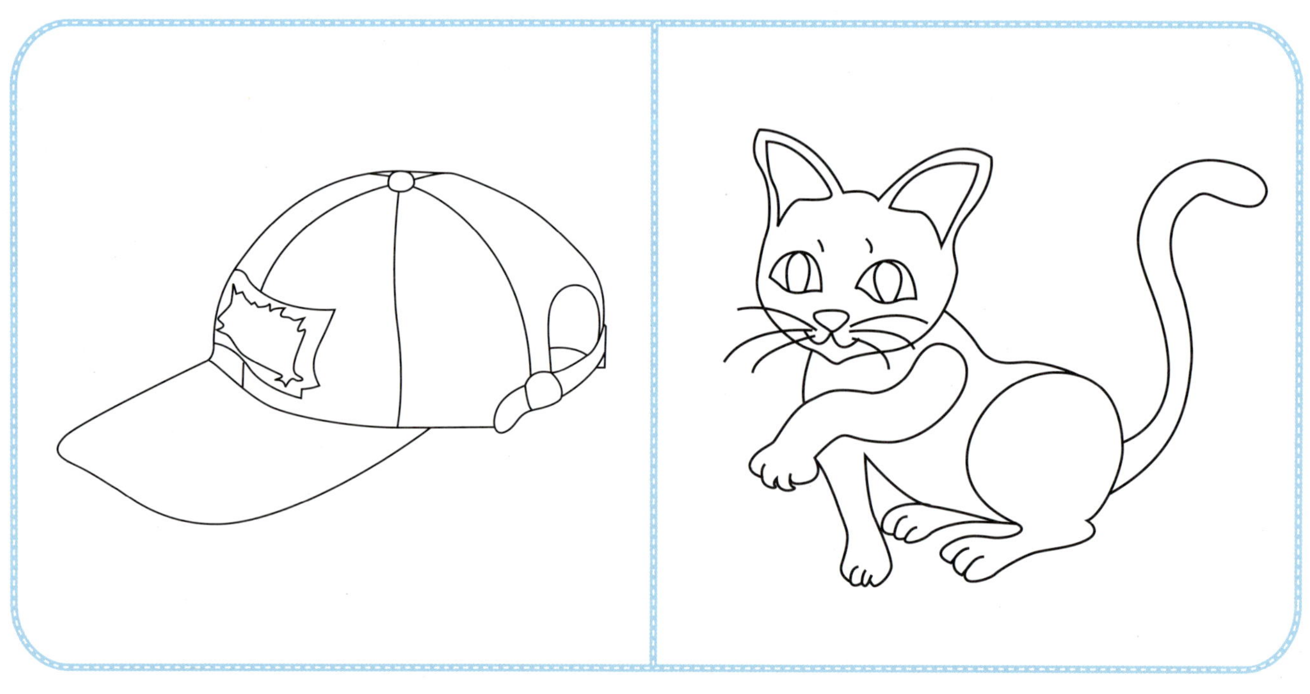

This is a tap / cap.

This is a cat / mat.

E Complete the words.

t_______

m_______

b_______

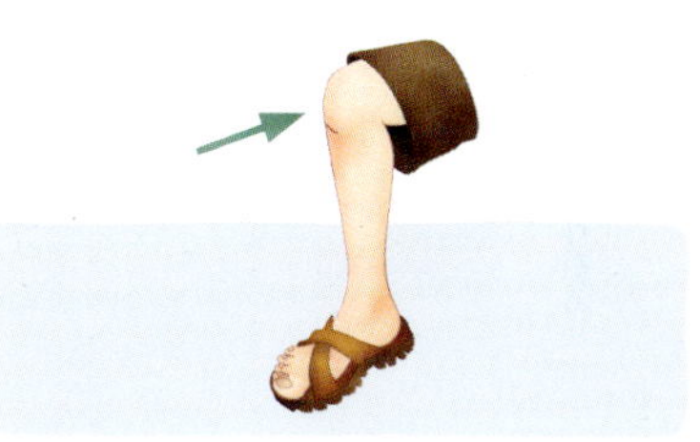

l_______

c_______

m_______

c_______

h_______

UNIT 4

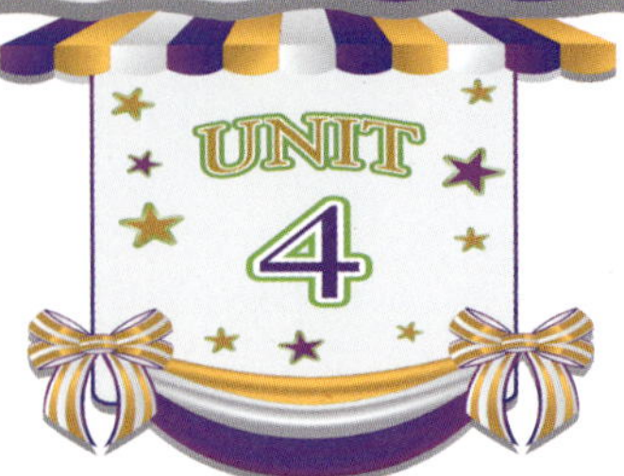

-ed -eg

A Choose and write.

T	r	w	b

+

ed

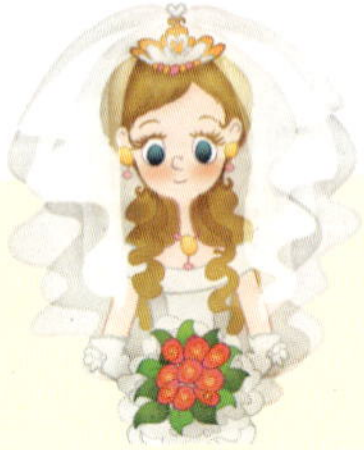

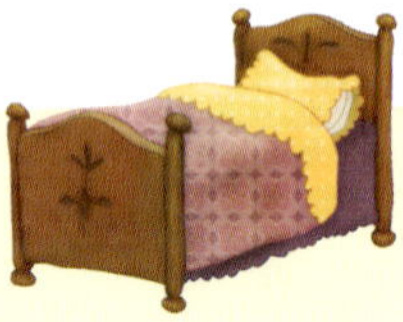

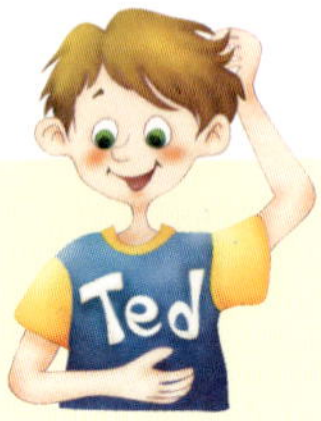

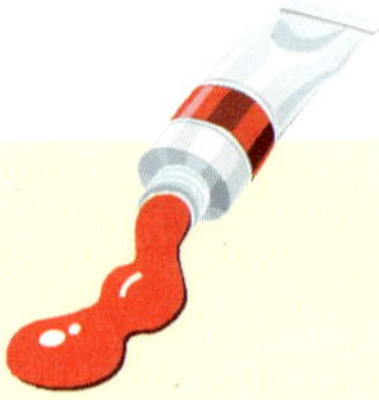

B Choose and write.

b p l ø

+

eg

_____ g

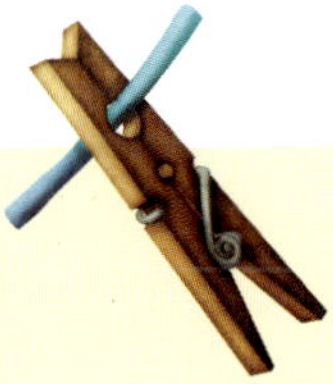

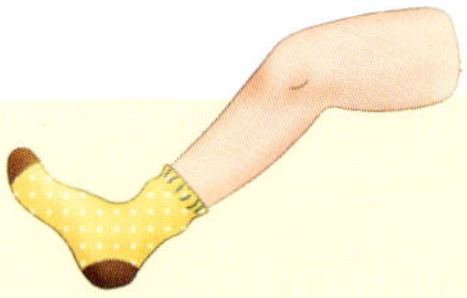

_____

_____

_____

 Circle the correct words.

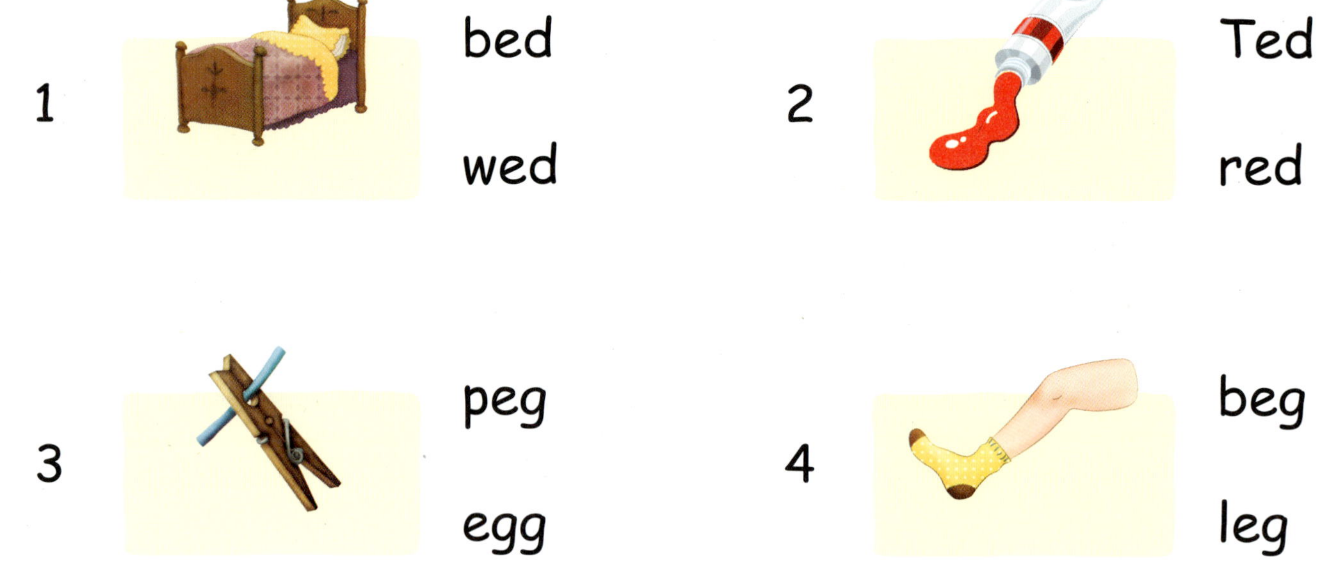

1. bed / wed

2. Ted / red

3. peg / egg

4. beg / leg

 Circle the correct word and color the picture.

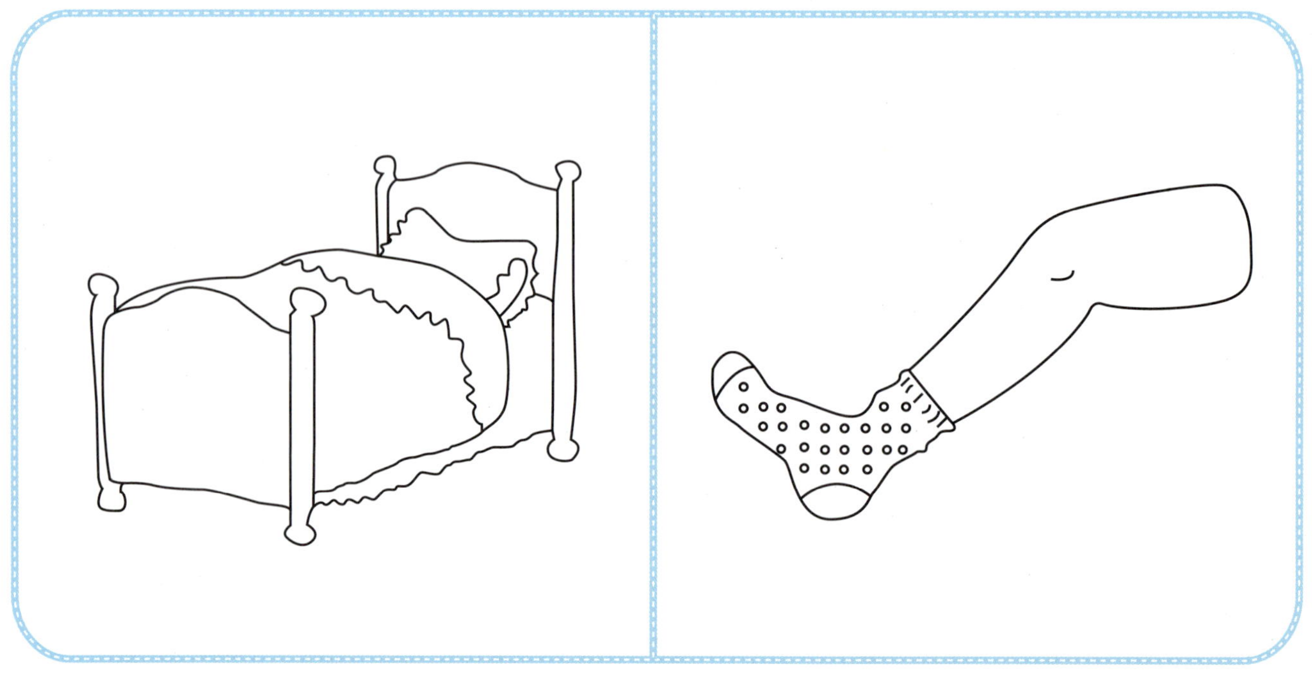

This is a bed / red.

This is a leg / peg.

E Complete the words.

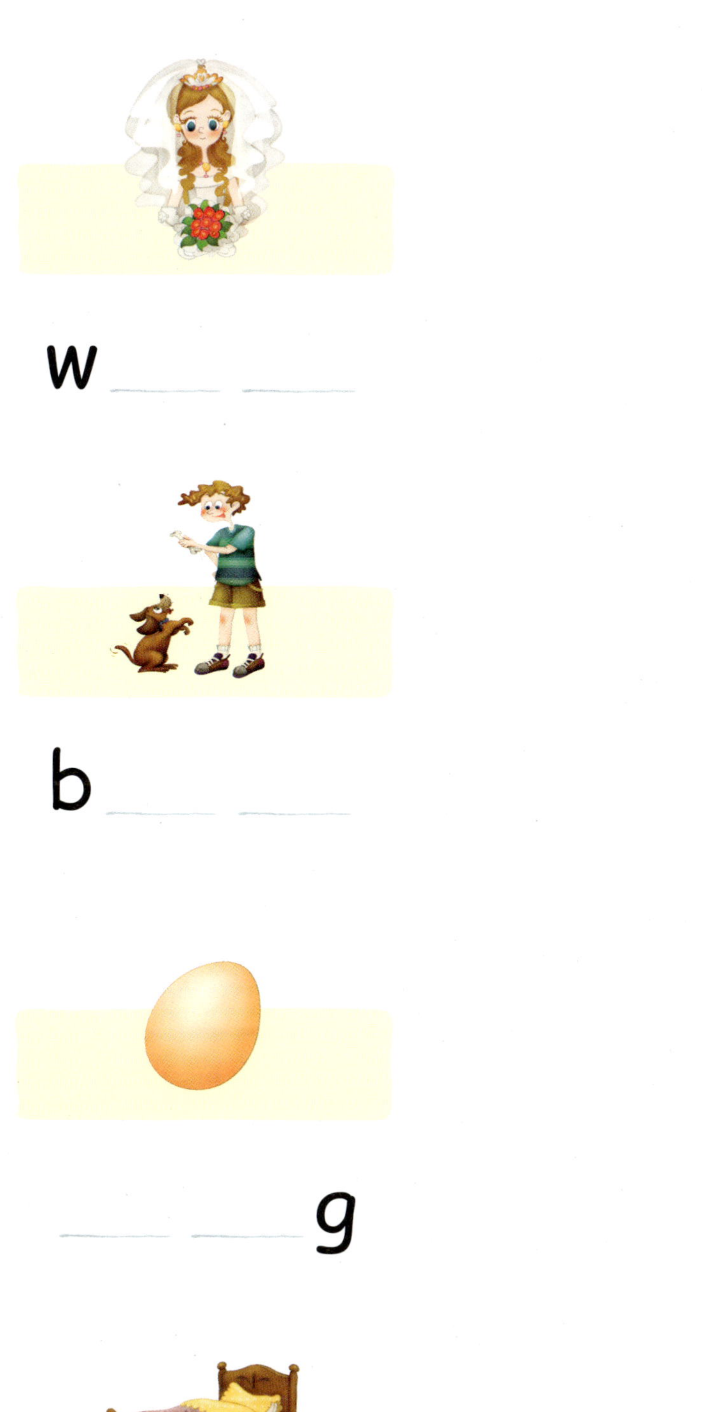

w _______   p _______

b _______   T _______

_______ g   r _______

b _______   l _______

-en   -et

A Choose and write.

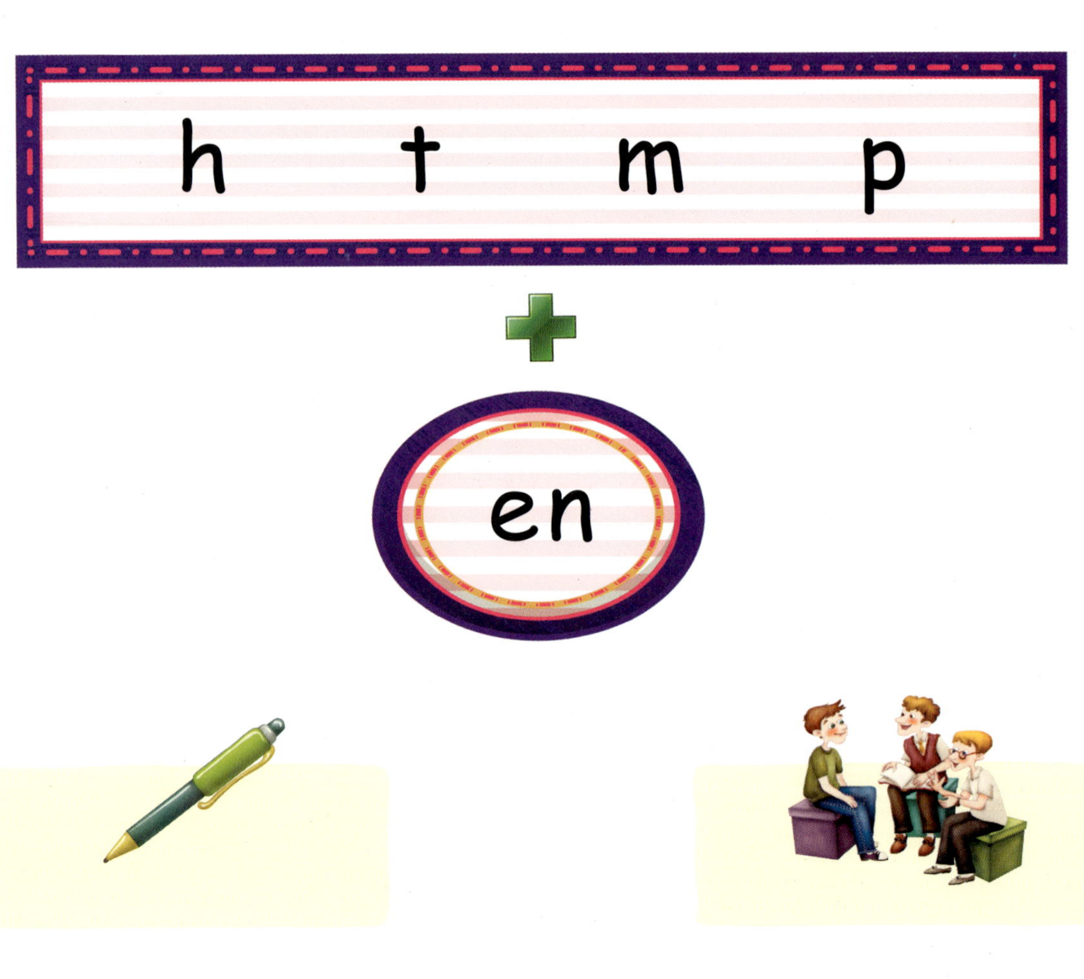

  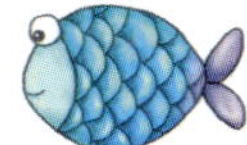    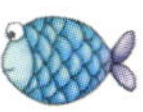

B Choose and write.

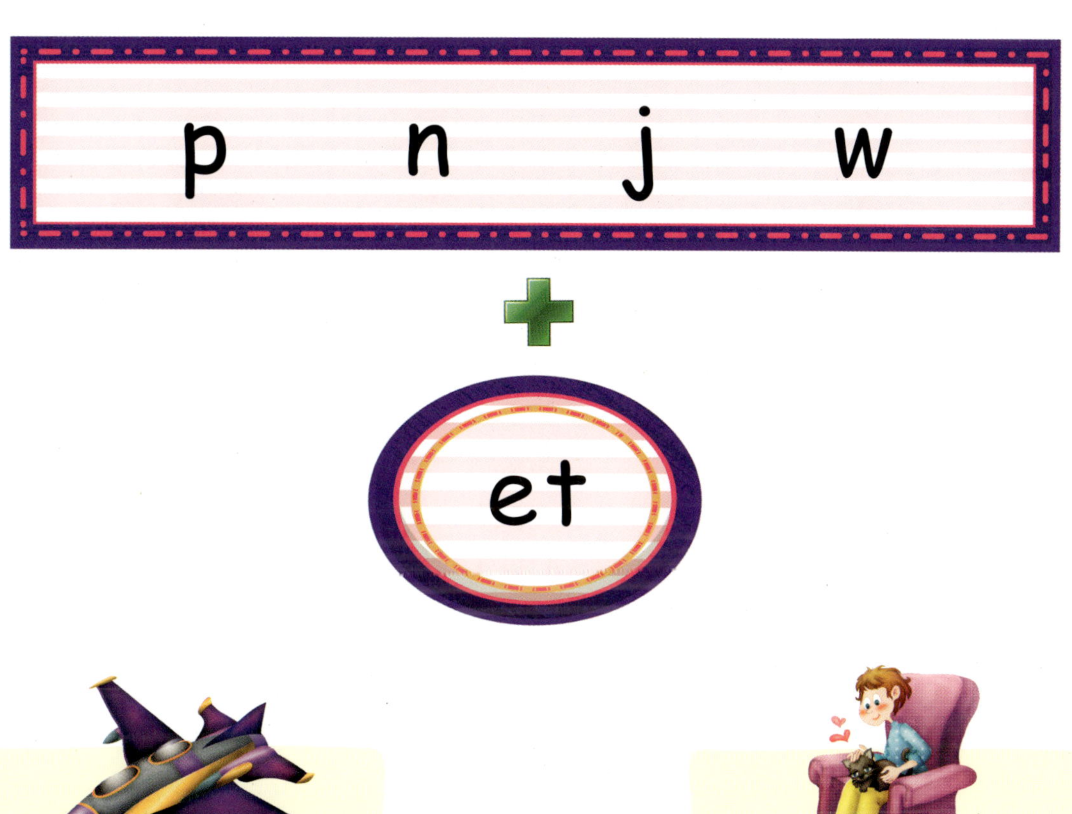

 Circle the correct words.

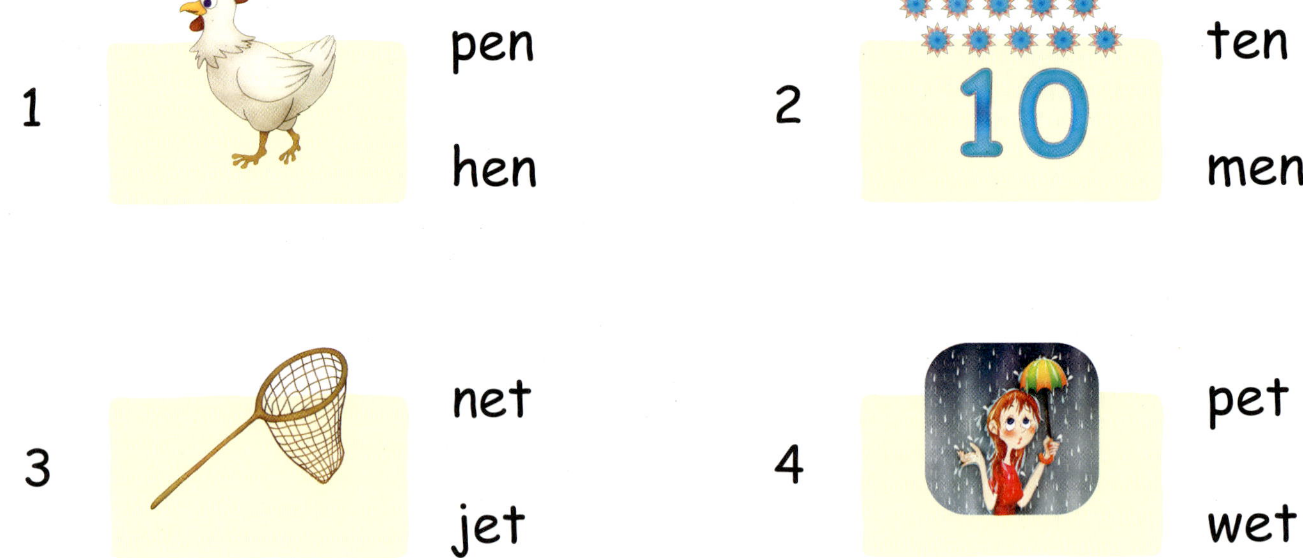

 Circle the correct word and color the picture.

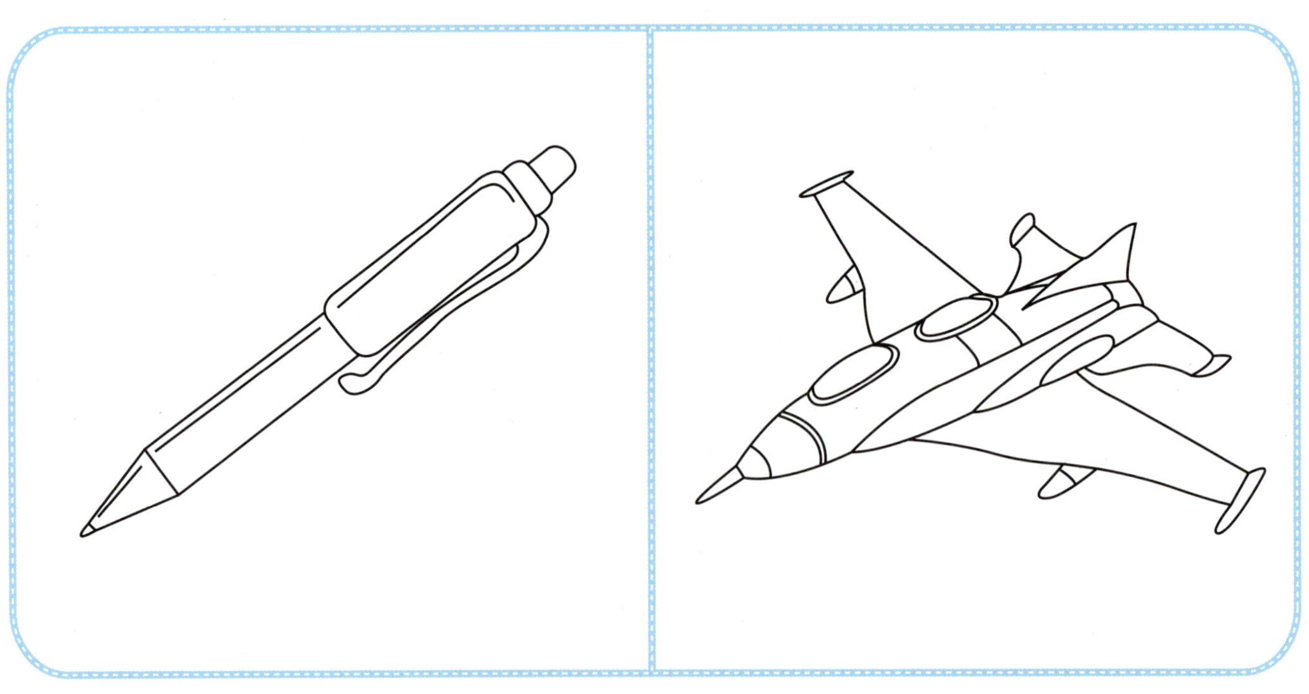

This is a hen / pen.

This is a jet / net.

E Complete the words.

j _________

m _________

t _________

p _________

h _________

w _________

n _________

p _________

-id   -ig

A Choose and write.

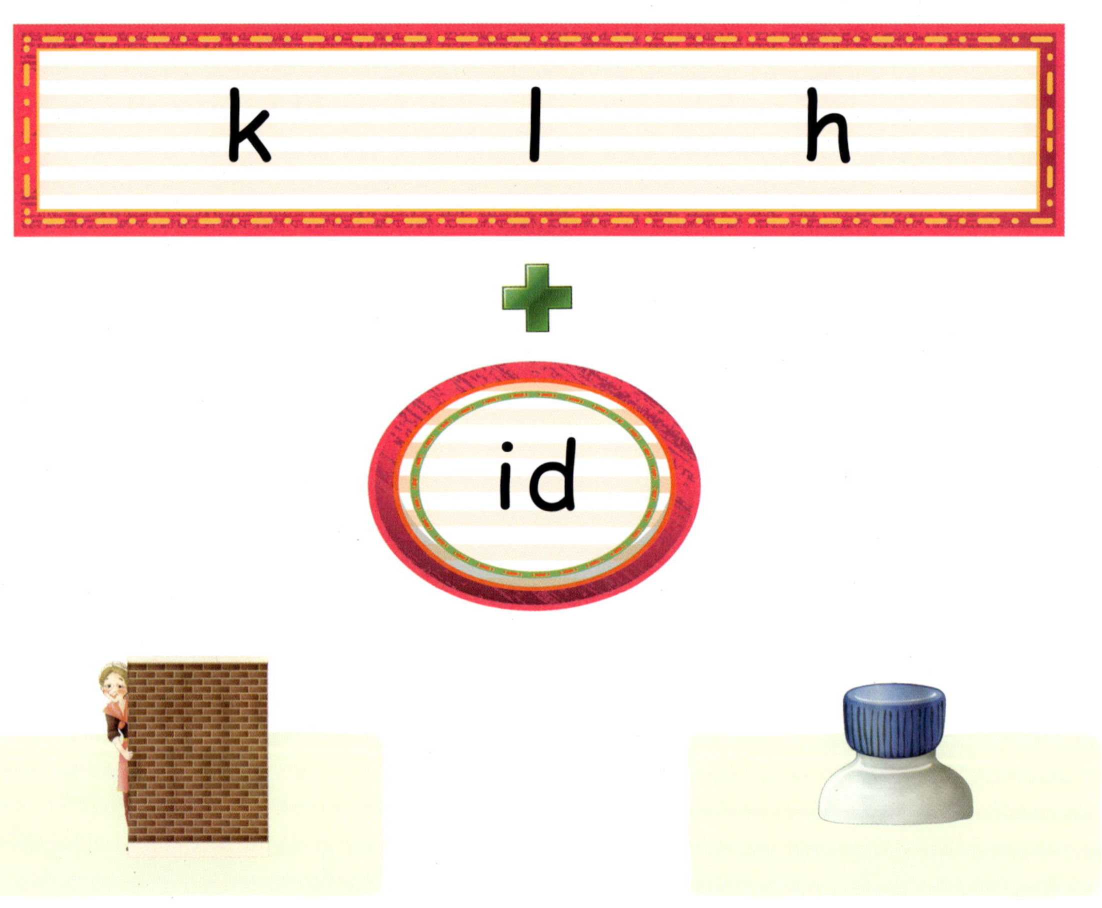

_________________   _________________

____

B Choose and write.

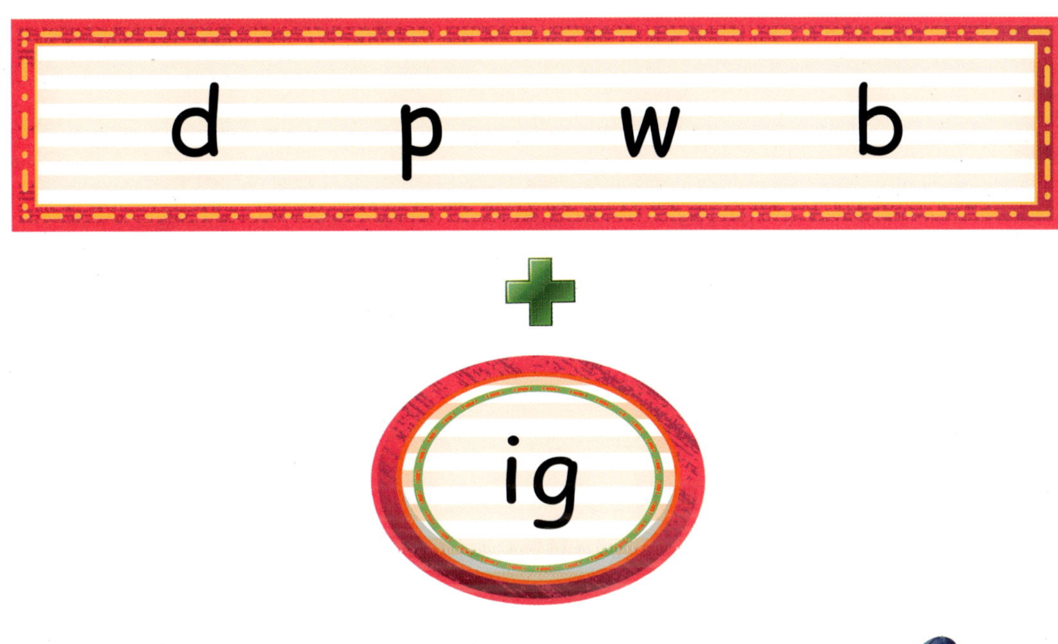

This is a lid / kid.   This is a wig / pig.

E Complete the words.

l _____

b _____

d _____

k _____

w _____

h _____

p _____

-in   -ip

 Choose and write.

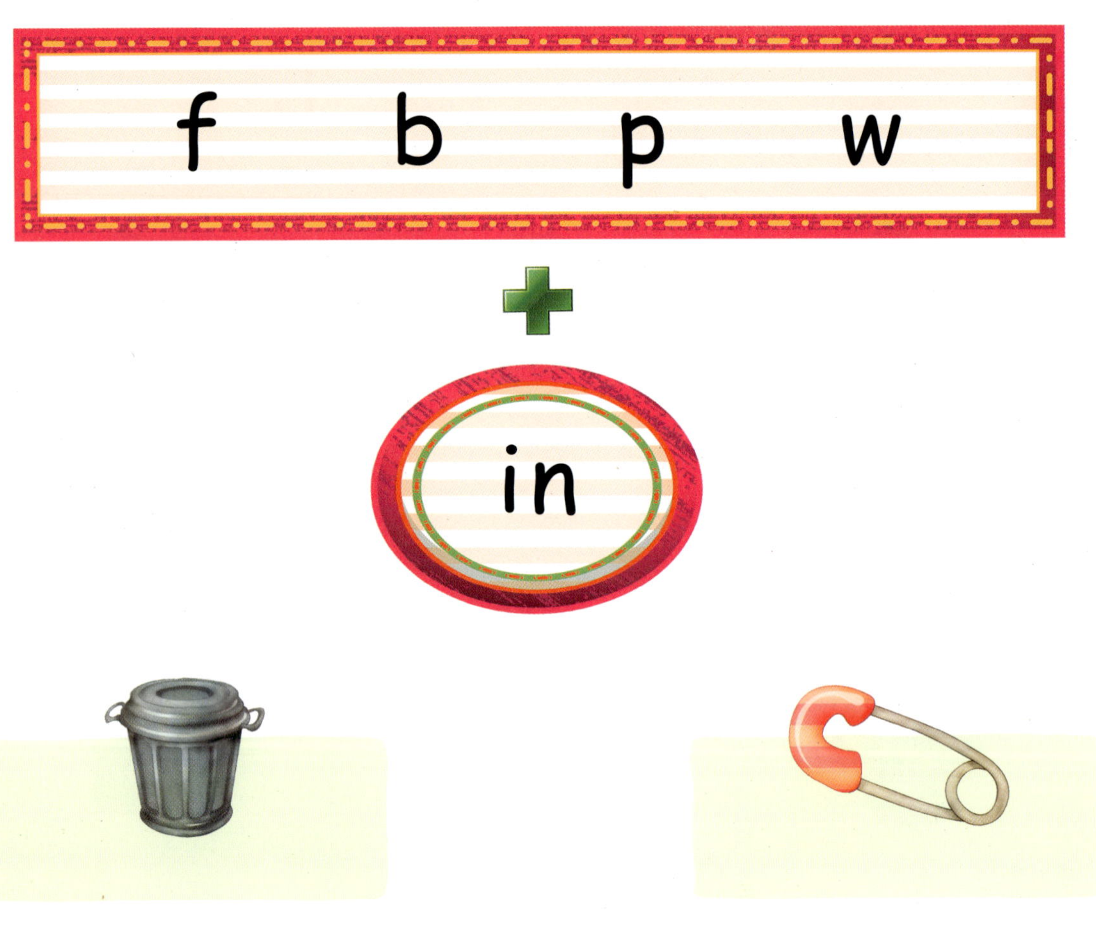

  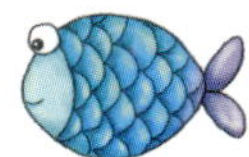    

B Choose and write.

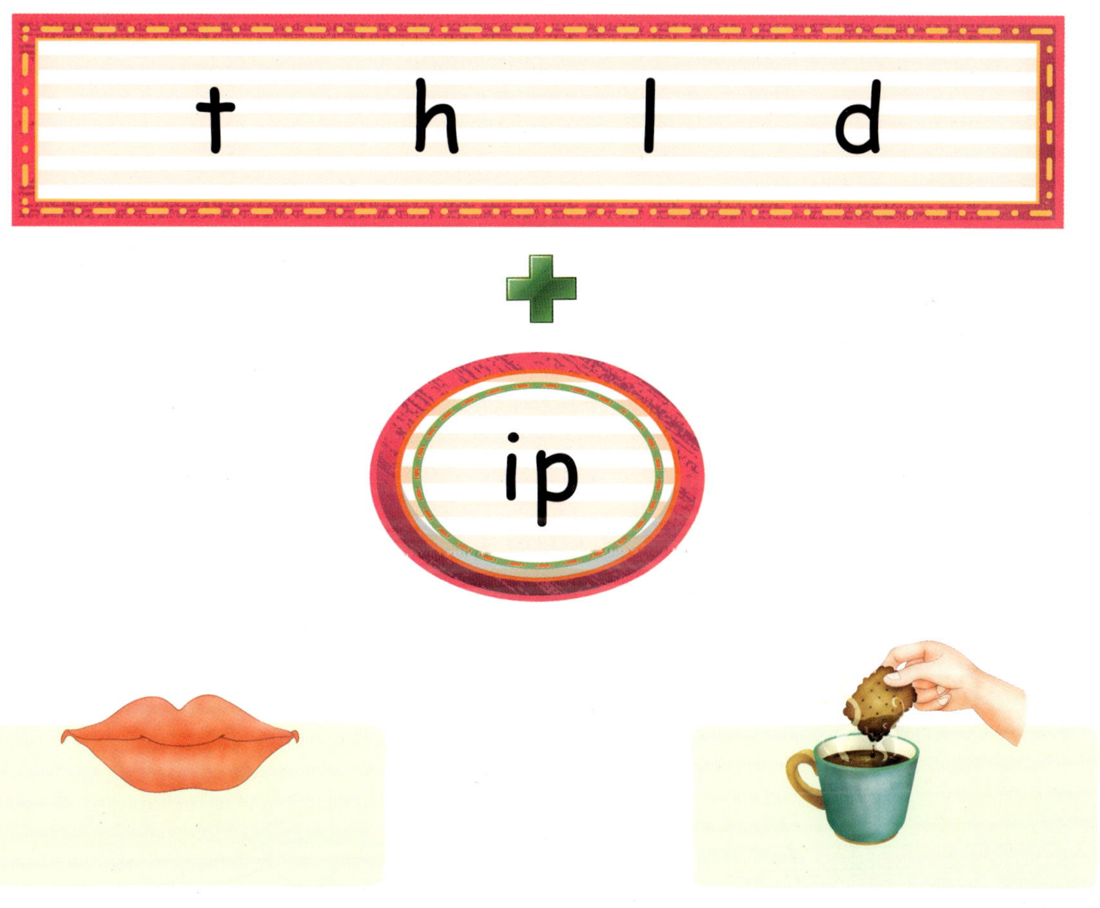

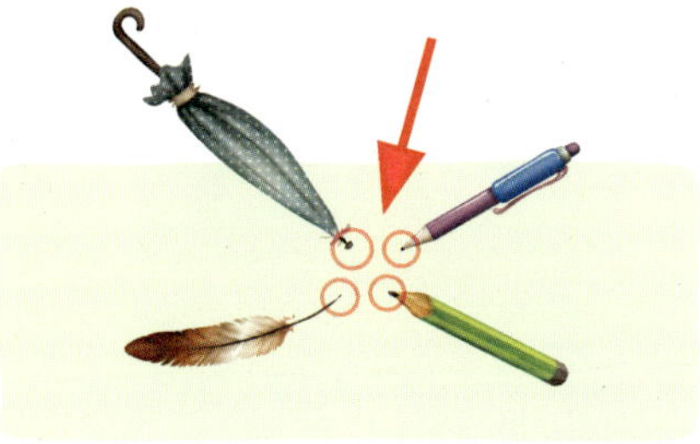

Circle the correct words.

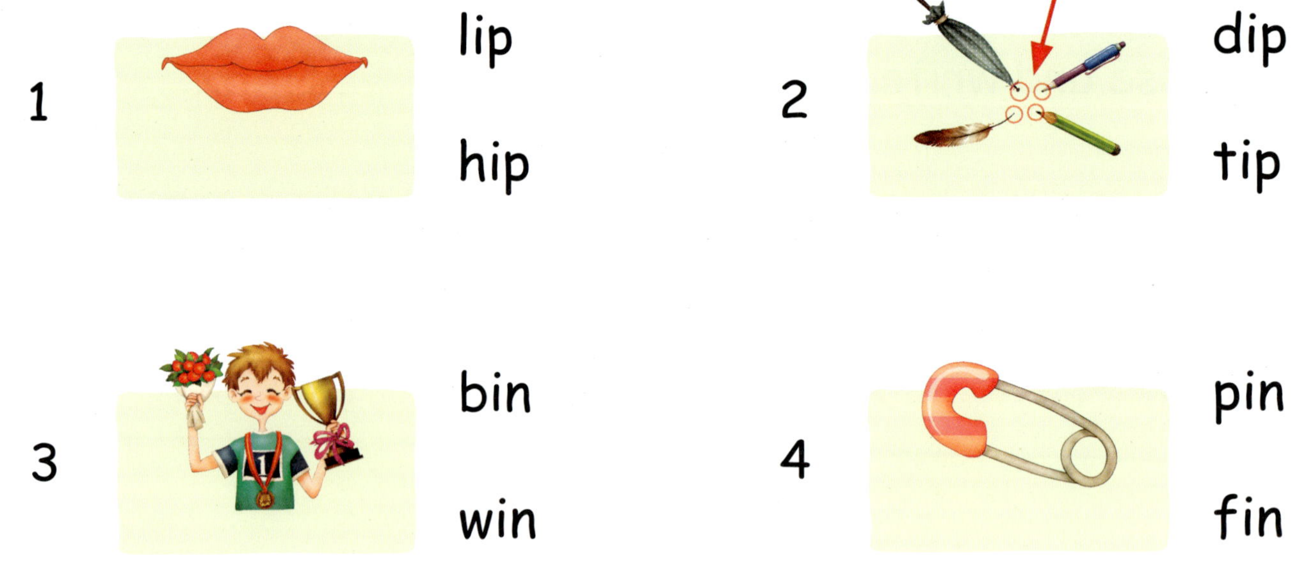

1   lip / hip

2   dip / tip

3   bin / win

4   pin / fin

Circle the correct word and color the picture.

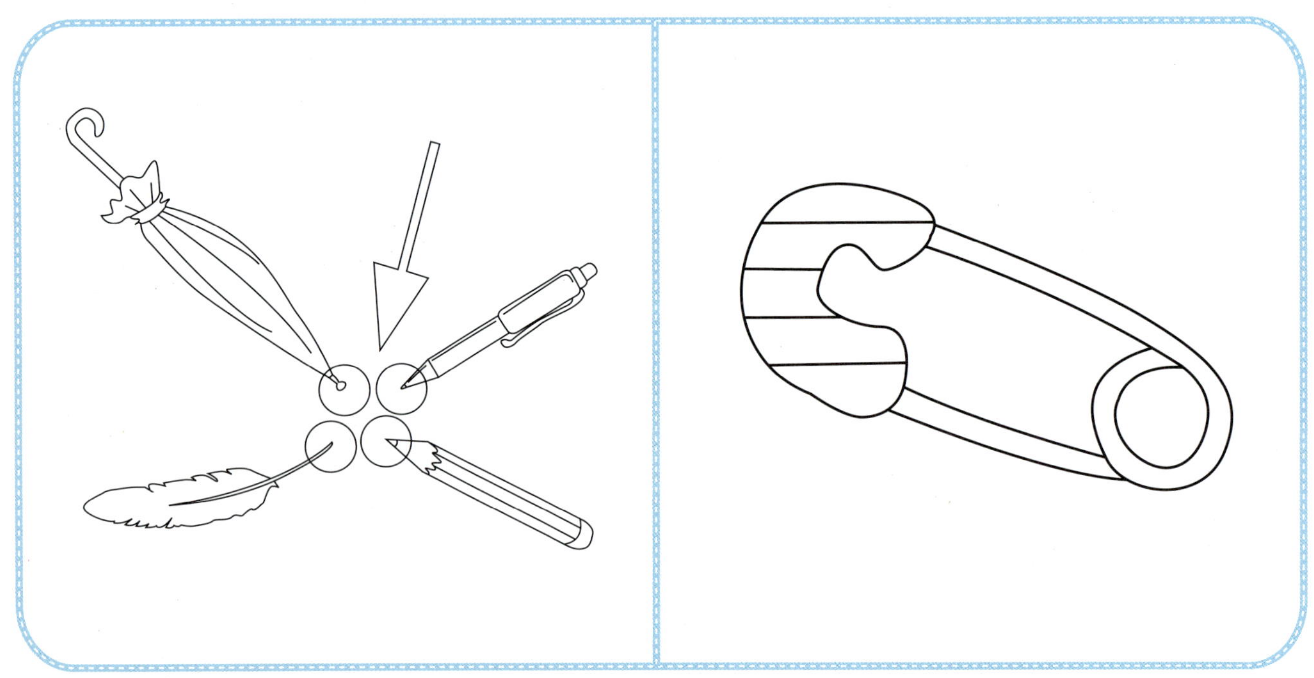

This is the lip / tip.

This is a pin / bin.

E Complete the words.

d _ _ _

f _ _ _

w _ _ _

h _ _ _

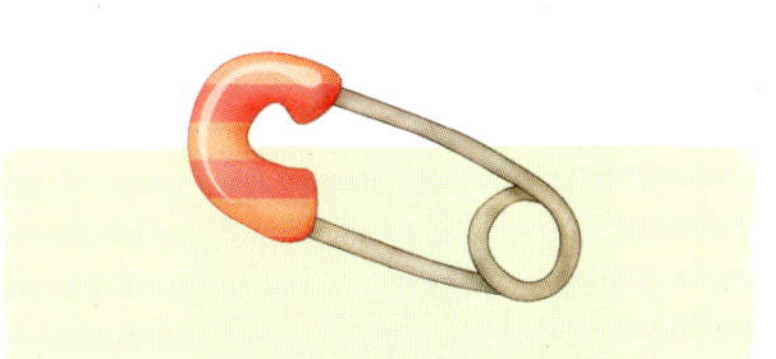

p _ _ _

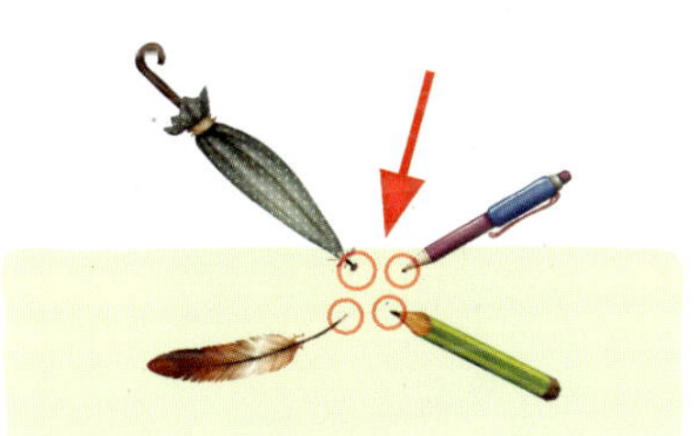

t _ _ _

l _ _ _

b _ _ _

UNIT 8

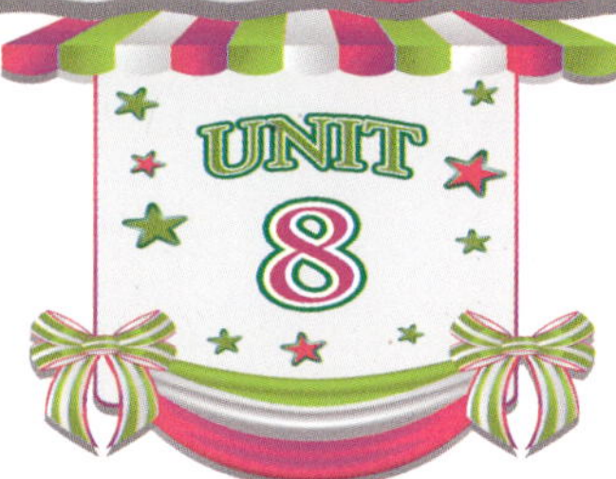

-it -ix

A Choose and write.

s h p f

+

it

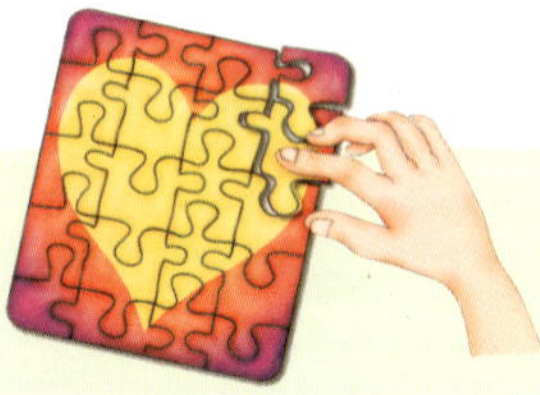

______

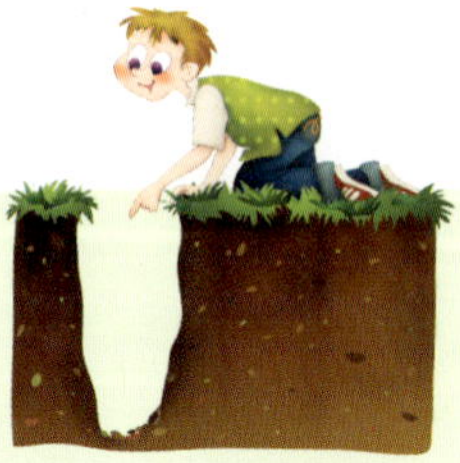

______

______

______

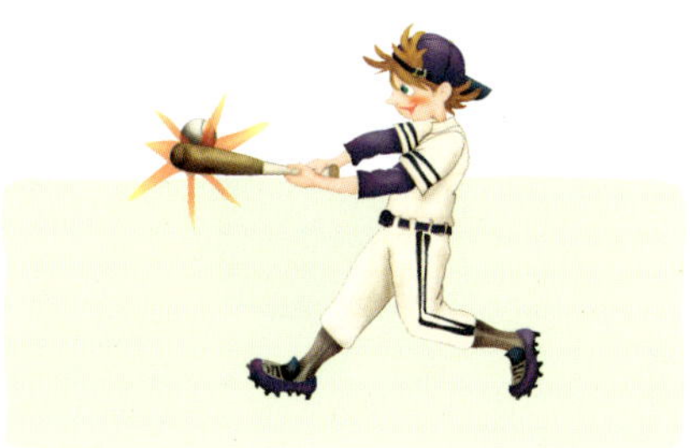

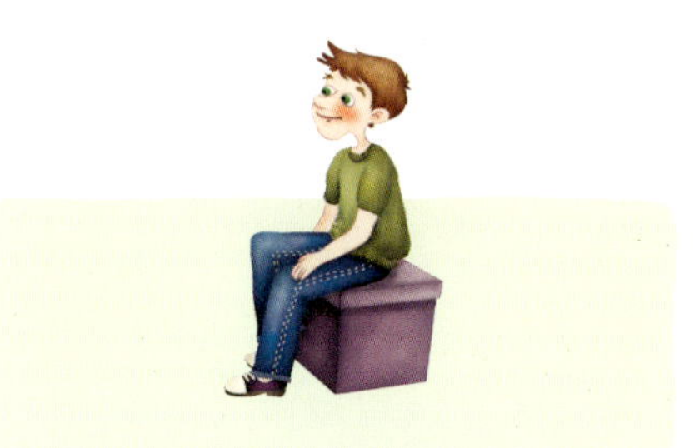

  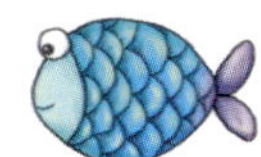    

B **Choose and write.**

Circle the correct words.

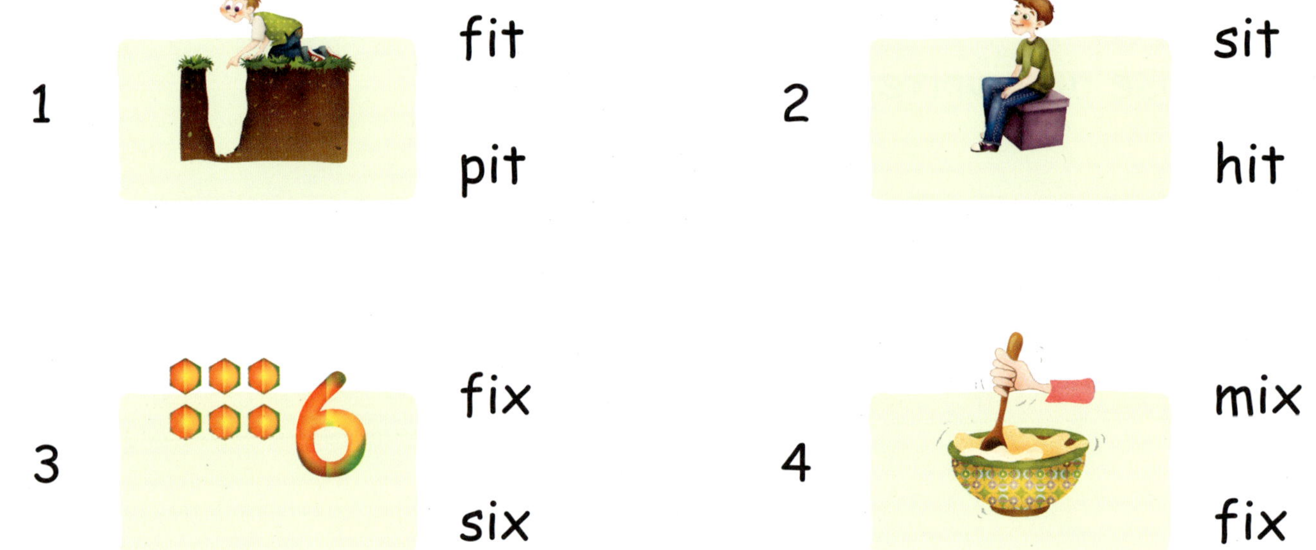

Circle the correct word and color the picture.

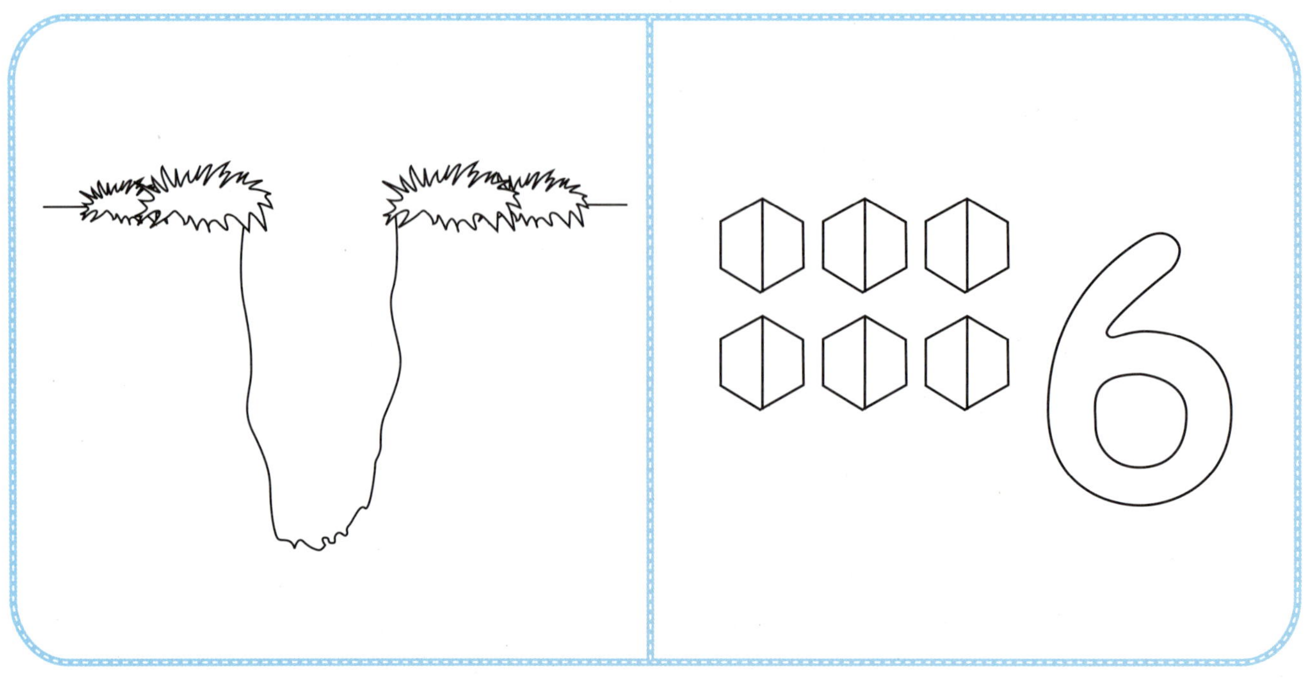

This is a pit / fit.

This is six / mix.

E Complete the words.

p _______

m _______

s _______

h _______

f _______

f _______

s _______

UNIT 9

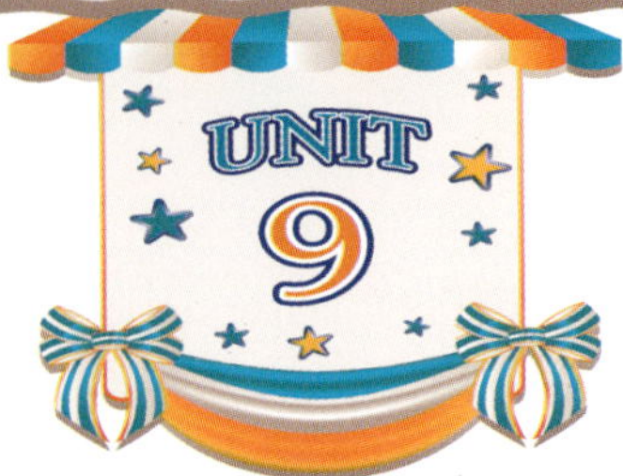

-og -op

A Choose and write.

f d l j

+

og

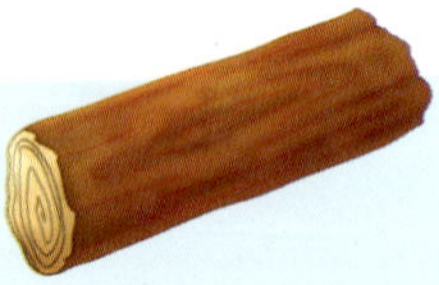

____

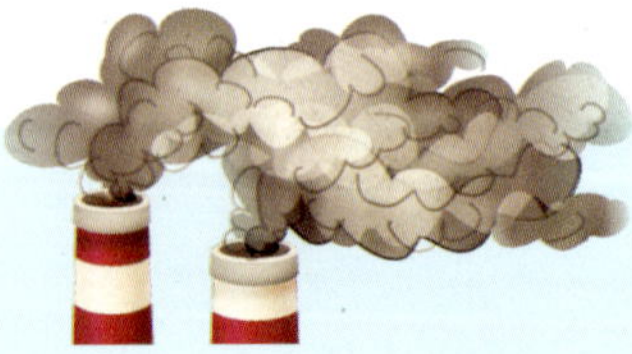

____

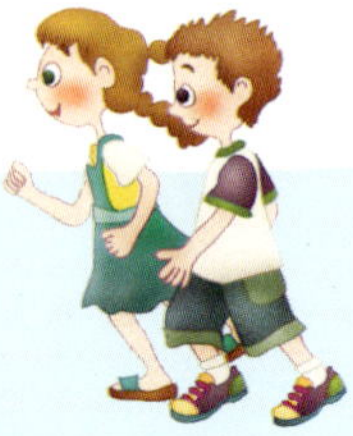

____

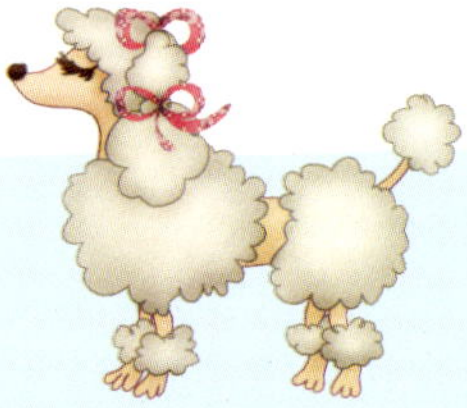

____

Ⓑ Choose and write.

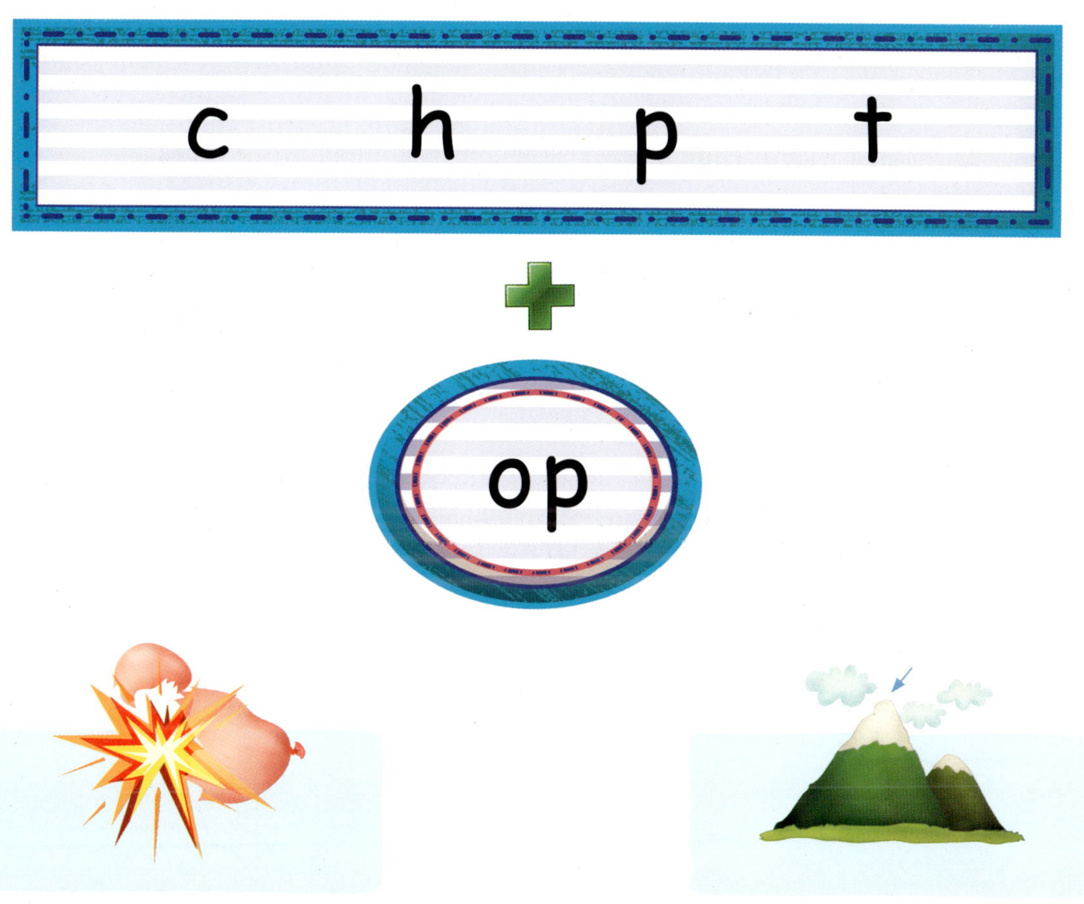

Circle the correct words.

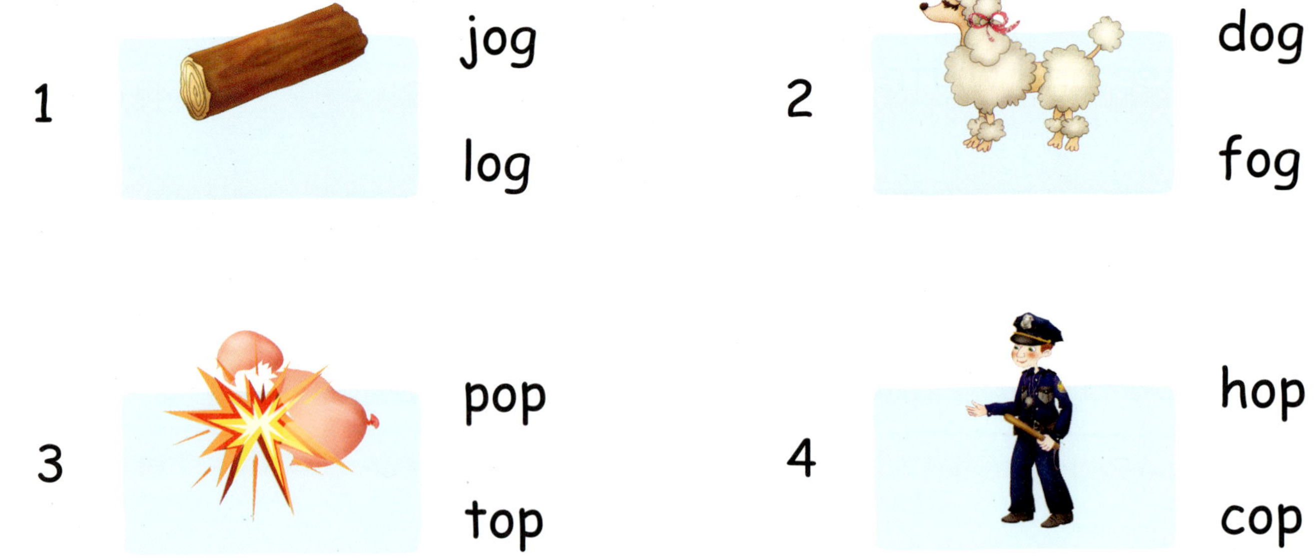

1 jog / log

2 dog / fog

3 pop / top

4 hop / cop

Circle the correct word and color the picture.

This is a dog / log.

This is the cop / top.

36

E Complete the words.

j 

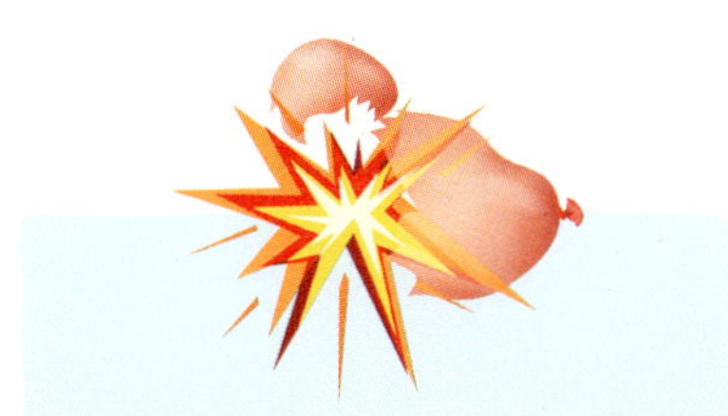

p _______

f _______

h 

c _______

l _______

t _______

d _______

-ot   -ox

A Choose and write.

d h p n

+

ot

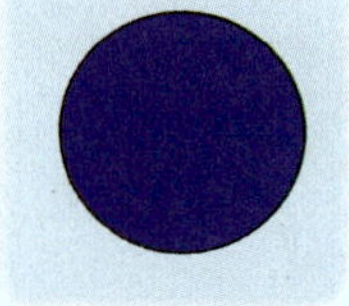

B Choose and write.

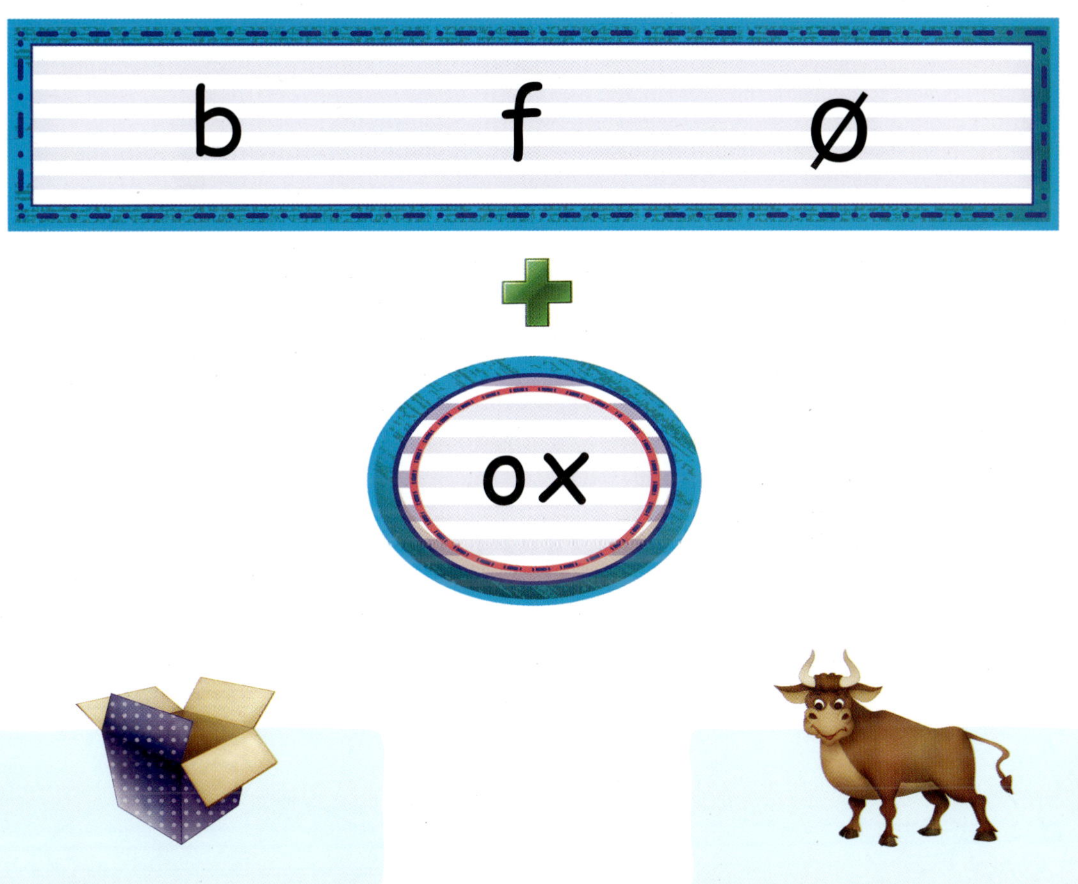

 Circle the correct words.

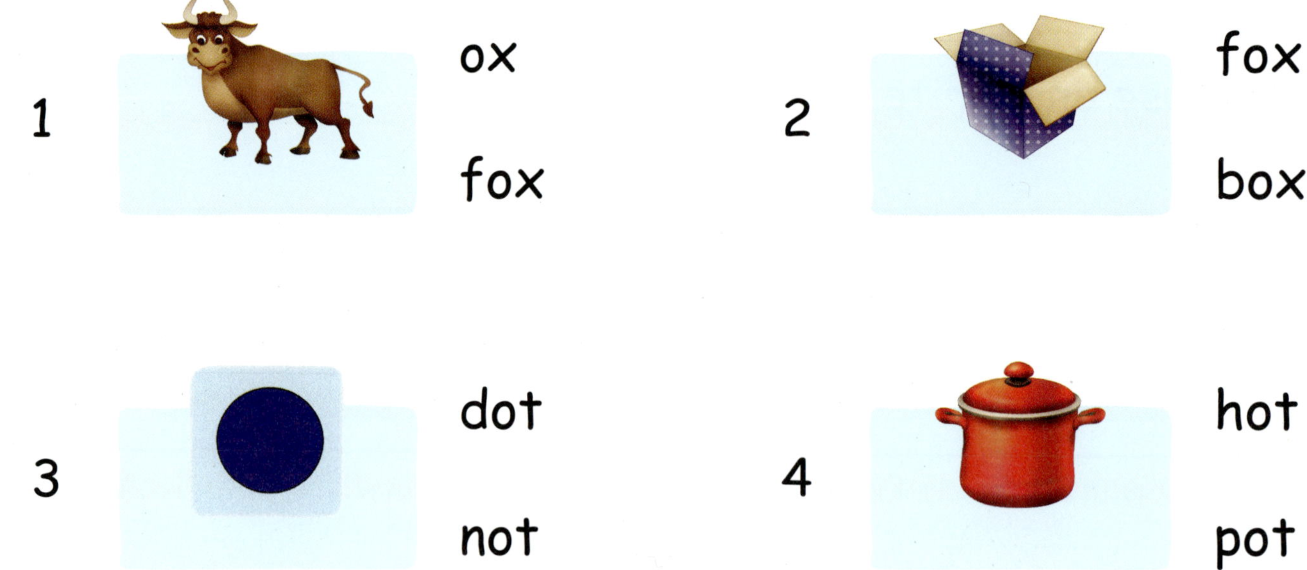

1   ox / fox

2   fox / box

3   dot / not

4   hot / pot

D Circle the correct word and color the picture.

This is a(n) ox / box.

This is a pot / dot.

 Complete the words.

h_______

f______

d______

b______

______

p_____

n______

-ug   -un

Ⓐ Choose and write.

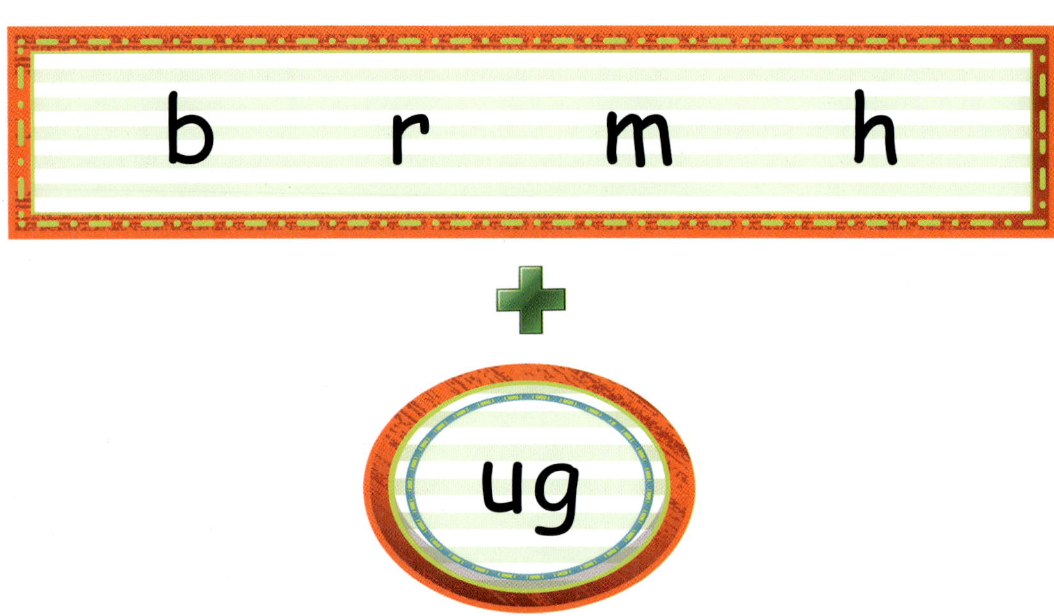

____

____

____

____

B Choose and write.

Circle the correct words.

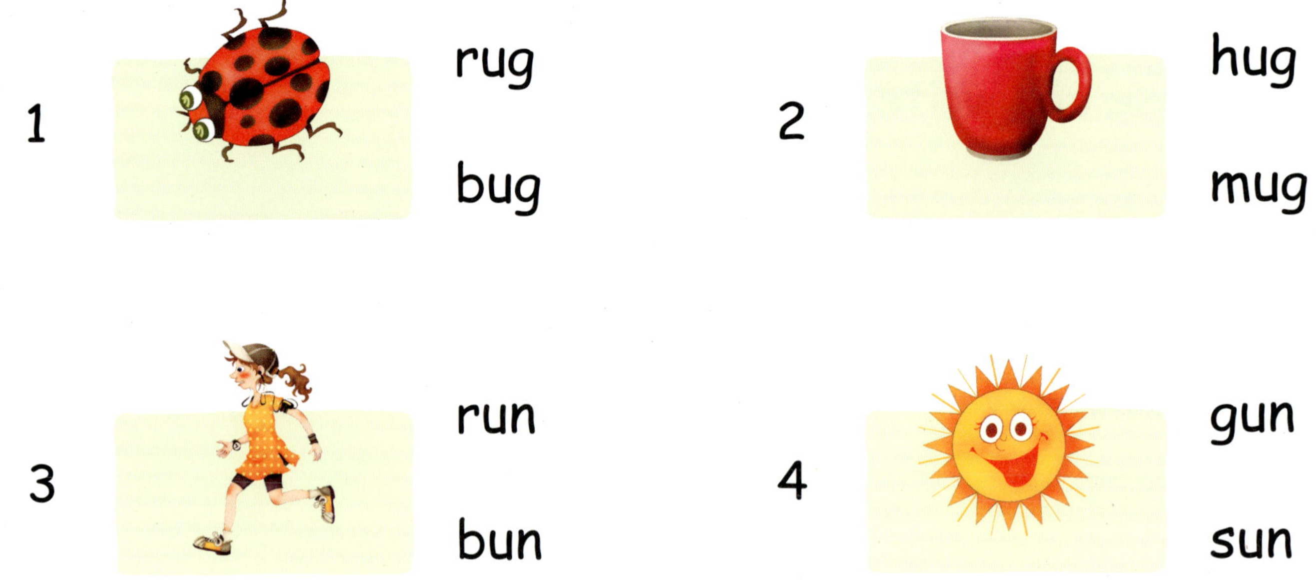

Circle the correct word and color the picture.

This is a mug / bug.

This is the sun / bun.

 Complete the words.

h _______

s _______

r _______

r _______

g _______

b _______

m _______

b _______

-up   -ut

A **Choose and write.**

B **Choose and write.**

Circle the correct words.

Circle the correct word and color the picture.

This is a hut / nut.

This is a pup / cup.

E Complete the words.

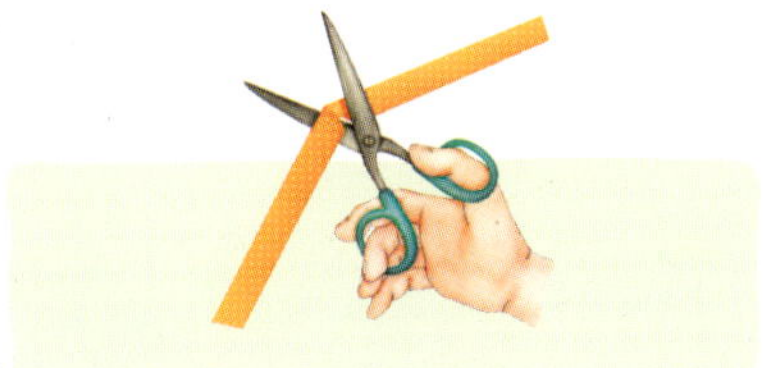

c _______

p _______

n _______

c _______

____

h _______

CERTIFICATE

Name

Date

Signed

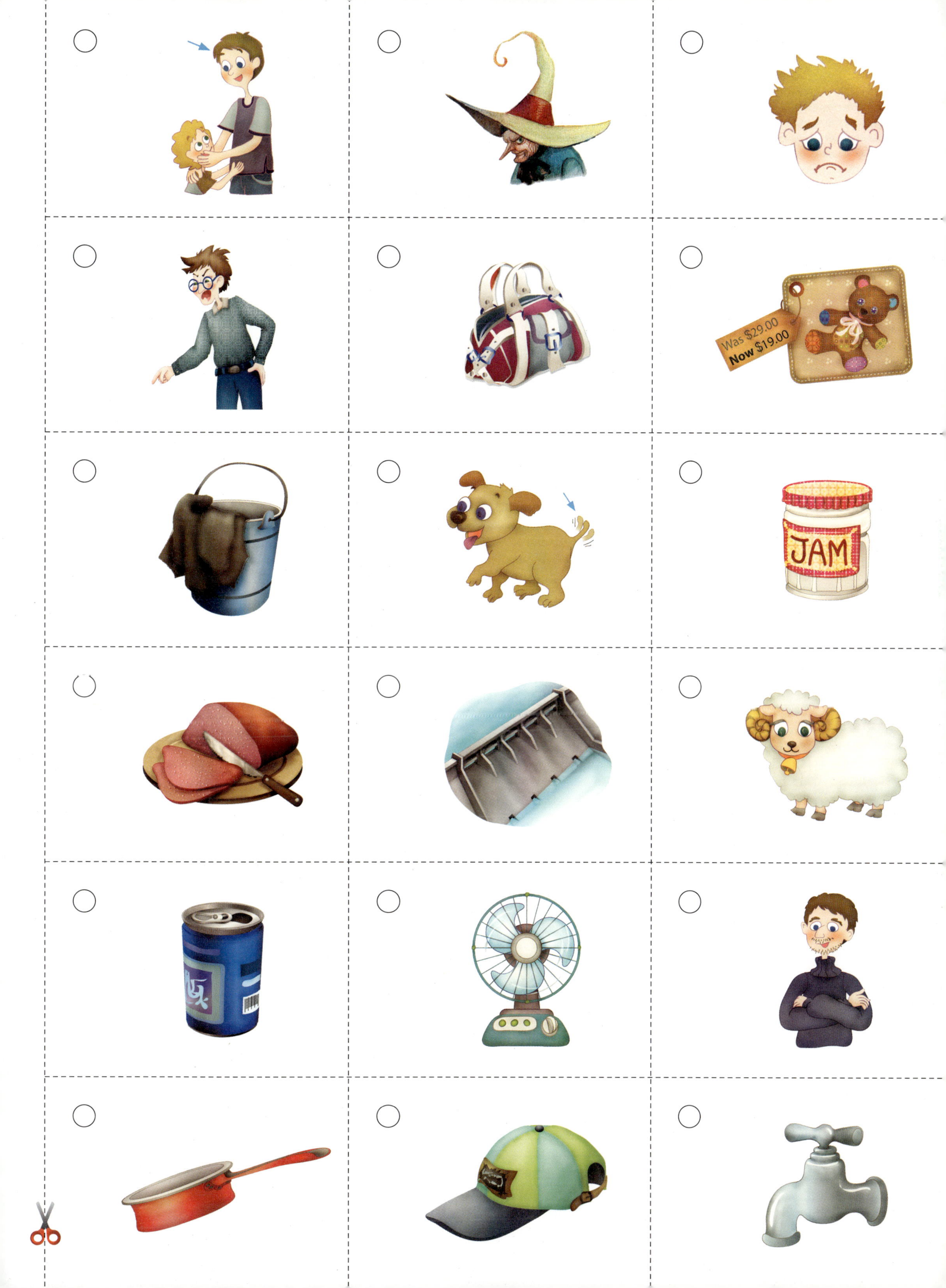
Was $29.00
Now $19.00
JAM

sad	bad	dad
tag	bag	mad
jam	wag	rag
ram	dam	ham
man	fan	can
tap	cap	pan

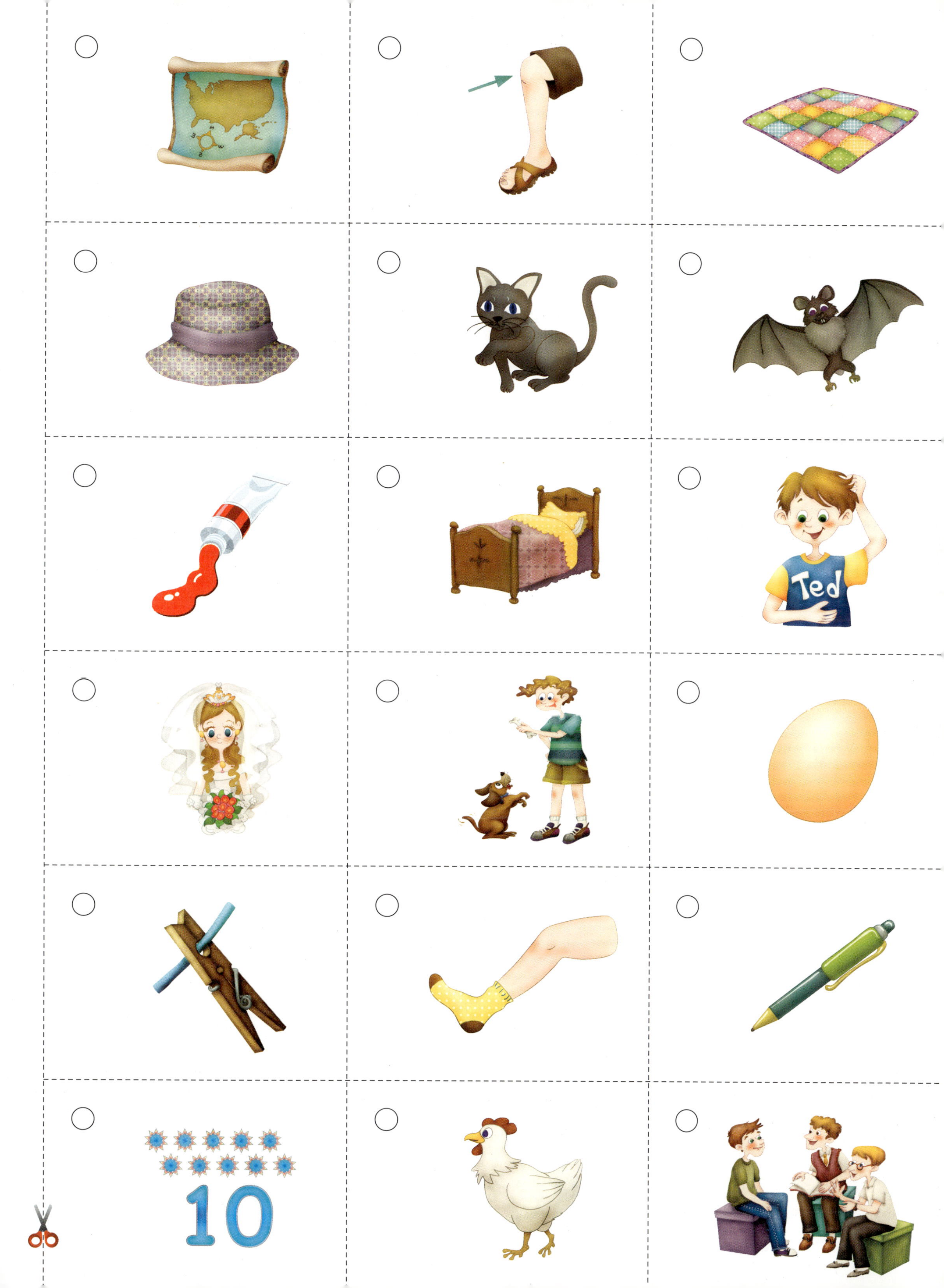

mat	lap	map
bat	cat	hat
Ted	bed	red
egg	beg	wed
pen	leg	peg
men	hen	ten

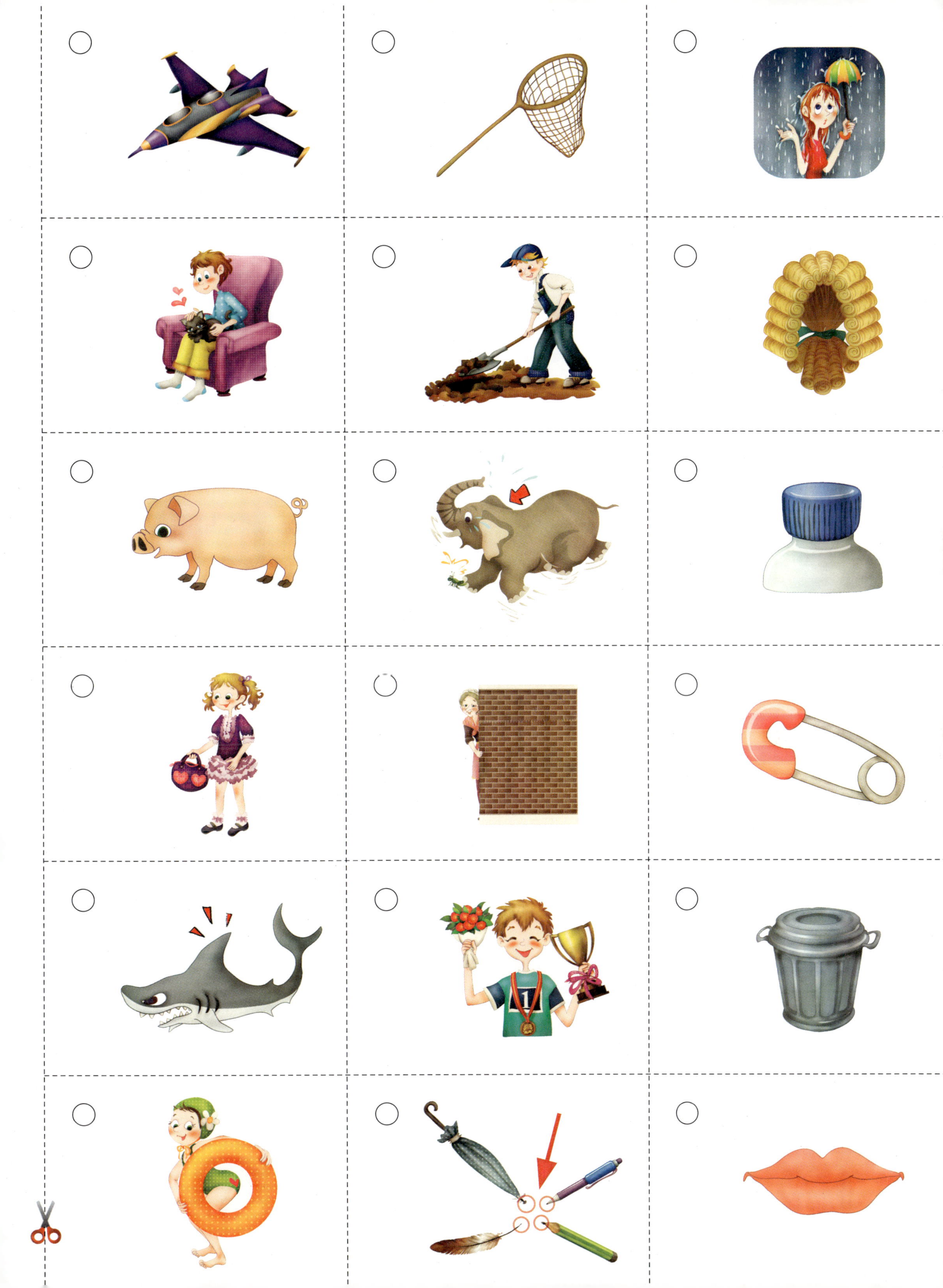

wet	net	jet
wig	dig	pet
lid	big	pig
pin	hid	kid
bin	win	fin
lip	tip	hip

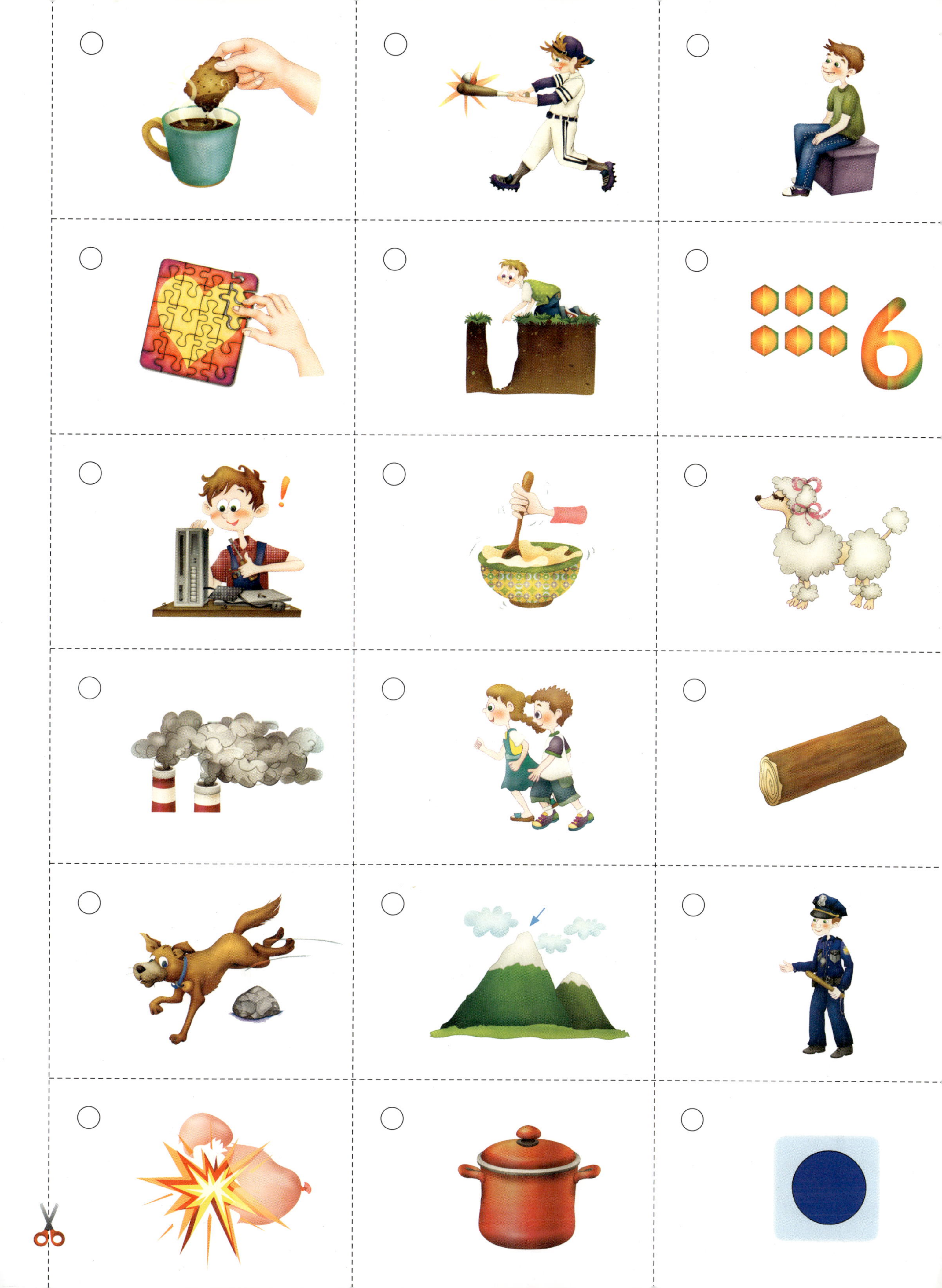

sit	hit	dip
six	pit	fit
dog	mix	fix
log	jog	fog
cop	top	hop
dot	pot	pop

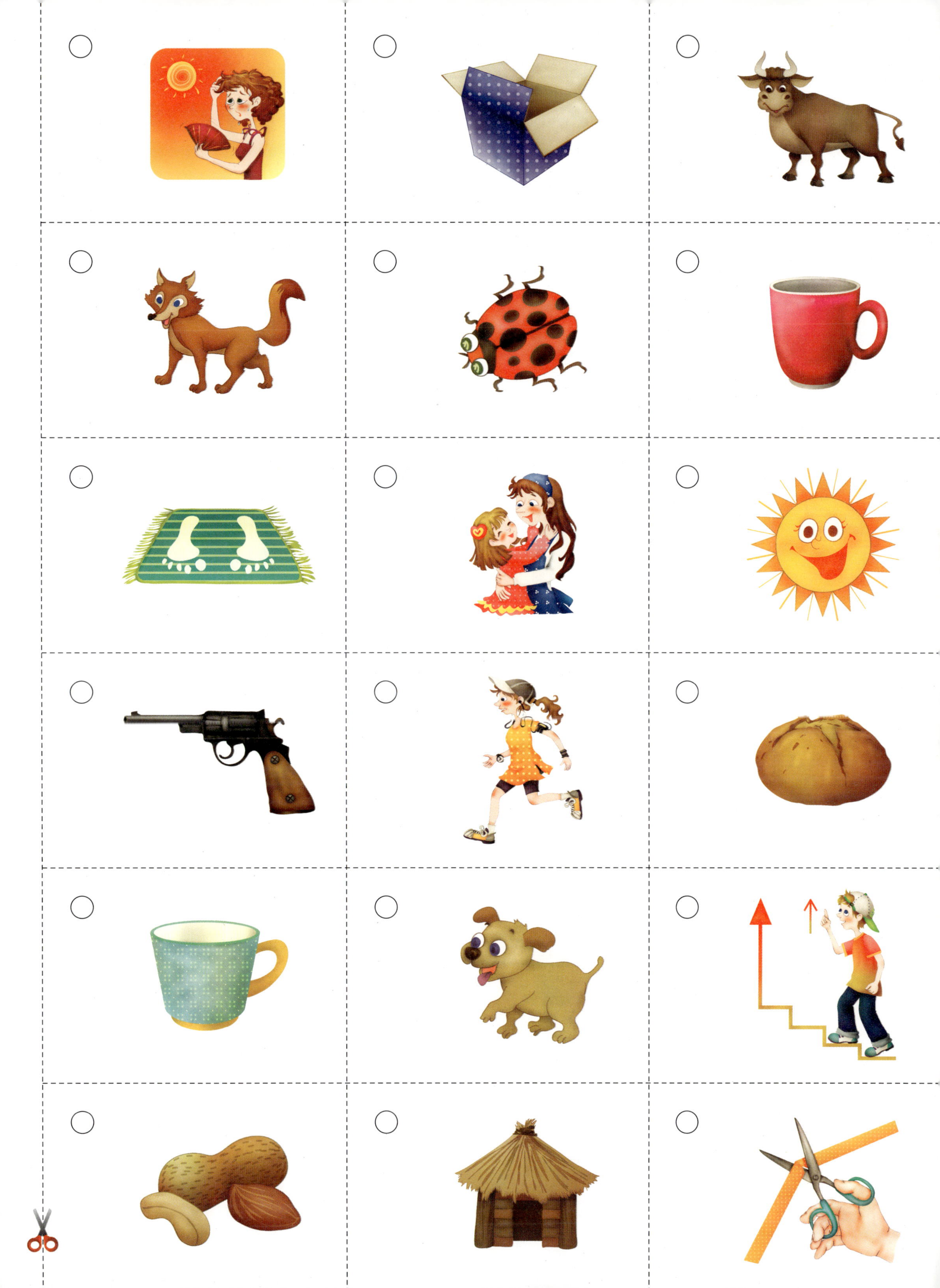

ox	box	hot
mug	bug	fox
sun	hug	rug
bun	run	gun
up	pup	cup
cut	hut	hut